FEAR DAT

NEW ORLEANS

A Guide to the Voodoo, Vampires,
Graveyards & Ghosts of the Crescent City

MICHAEL MURPHY

THE COUNTRYMAN PRESS
WOODSTOCK, VT

Published by The Countryman Press
www.countrymanpress.com

A division of W. W. Norton & Company, Inc.,
500 Fifth Avenue, New York, NY 10110
www.wwnorton.com

For information about special discounts for bulk purchases, please contact
W. W. Norton Special Sales at specialsales@wwnorton.com or 800-233-4830.

Printed in the United States
978-1-58157-275-9

0 9 8 7 6 5 4 3 2 1

FEAR DAT
NEW ORLEANS

To write something you have to risk making a fool of yourself.
—Anne Rice

I dedicated my previous book, *Eat Dat*, to the city of New Orleans, which I said feeds me every day. For *Fear Dat*, I again dedicate the book to the city of New Orleans, which seduces, baffles, excites, and sometimes tests me or scares me on a regular basis. In writing *Fear Dat*, I have met many new-to-me psychics, cemetery guides, and ghost hunters. Through these unique people, my love for New Orleans has grown even deeper.

Last Ride

Amy Brassette

CONTENTS

Jackson Square   ROB WEBSTER

INTRODUCTION

Fear makes us feel our humanity. —Benjamin Disraeli

Do one thing every day that scares you. —Eleanor Roosevelt

L ike more and more of us, I work multiple jobs not so much stay afloat as to drown at a more leisurely pace. My pay-the-electric-bill job is working behind the concierge desk at a large hotel. At least once a week—and usually far more often—guests new to New Orleans will ask me, "Is it safe to walk around?" or a companion question, "Where should I *not* go?" My pat, failed attempts at humorous answers are, respectively, "Just HOW do you walk?" and "Chicago." Then, I will mix in some partial truths to comfort them. New Orleans' crime rate was down 20 percent last year (true, if you believe the numbers the city police put forward). The year before, we had only the 13th-highest murder rate among US cities. Nothing to be proud of, but at least we're not in the top 10.

Behind my bad jokes and patchwork facts, I am seething. I love New Orleans. I hate the way the media creates a false image and then feeds it with further half-truths in order to prop up their created misinformation.

Several years ago, two street punks were shot to death here on Halloween night. National headlines the next day read, "Two Shot Dead in New Orleans Halloween Night." The same night, five were shot dead in Washington, DC. Nothing.

Colin Cowherd, the ESPN spew-caster who was voted Asshole of the Year and Douche Bag of the Year by two different polls and in two different years, descended into an on-air rant when the NFL was considering moving the Pro Bowl from Hawaii to New Orleans. He raged that New Orleans was a terrible choice because it's the Murder Capital (wrong), and since the Pro Bowl is in early February, you'd never want take your family to New Orleans during Mardi Gras (also wrong).

Often I feel the best way to engage with idiots is not to confront them, but to seduce them. So, I got my hotel to agree to provide Colin with free accommodations for Mardi Gras, and I approached the Krewe of Barkus, an annual Mardi Gras parade of dogs in costume, to have Colin Cowherd as its grand marshal. He could ride the parade inside a much deserved doghouse. I felt that if he actually experienced New Orleans in Mardi Gras season, he'd have a much harder time holding to his bogus beliefs. Unfortunately, Colin failed to respond to my several requests that he join us. Why let real life get in the way of wrongly held opinions?

One of my favorite moments in TV history was watching the Weather Channel's storm tracker, Jim Cantore, get exposed. He was huddled inside a hooded parka, seemingly battling hurricane-force winds and barely able to stand in one place. Then, two people in bathing suits casually sauntered behind him, giving the camera their best WTF looks.

So, on the one hand, I want to be the bathing-suited saunterers and convince would-be visitors that New Orleans is safe—well, relatively. As in any American city, you can get in trouble here. But statistically we are safer than Chicago, Philadelphia, Baltimore, Oakland, Tampa, Memphis, Oklahoma City . . . I could go on. I doubt if concierges in Tampa and Oklahoma City are asked on a weekly basis, "Is it safe to walk around?"

On the other hand, I do want to lure a certain type of visitor to New Orleans because we do have seductively dark corners to explore. We may not be the Murder Capital of America, but we are the Ghost, Voodoo, and Vampire Capital.

At the beginning of *Eat Dat*, the first of my New Orleans traveler's trilogy, I wrote: "At the risk of annoying every potential reader who doesn't live in or currently love New Orleans, I'm going to open by stating when it comes to food, New Orleans is the greatest city in America." Now I'll begin *Fear Dat* with a similar claim. When it comes to woo-woo, psychic, spiritual, otherworldly experiences, New Orleans is off the charts the woo-woo-iest city in America.

In *Eat Dat*, I cited endorsements from Anthony Bourdain, Mario Batali, and *Saveur* magazine to back up my claim of New Orleans' being the #1 food city in America. Here I will again use others to support my woo-woo-iest claim.

Gina Lanier, dubbed the Ghost Hunter's Ghost Hunter, is a well-established and nationally recognized paranormal investigator. When asked in an interview on her website, "Where is the most haunted city in America?" she replied, "New Orleans, Louisiana, by far. I have traveled the United States and it seems that southern ghosts are more apt to come out and show themselves more readily. Southern haunted hospitality, I guess."

Maria Shaw Lawson moved to New Orleans from Detroit because she and her husband, Joe, a paranormal investigator, were drawn in by the psychic energy of the place. She's now an internationally renowned psychic, founder of the annual Psychic Fair, and has ongoing gigs as the psychic scribe for *Soap Opera Digest* and the *National Enquirer*. In other words, hers is the only piece in the *Enquirer* that's not completely fabricated. Mary Shaw has said, "There's a spirit to this city. This city has a soul. If you can sense it, you don't want to go anywhere else."

But, more than psychic endorsements, just think about the tourists who come to New Orleans. In what other city can they stay at a haunted four-star hotel (Hotel Monteleone) or dine at a haunted four-star restaurant (Muriel's)? In what other city do tourists line up for cemetery visits and ghost tours as though they're waiting to see the *Mona Lisa* or climb the to the top of the Statue of Liberty?

It's a lesser-known fact that you can see zombie tourists on Decatur Street right in broad daylight. You can spot them in matching "I Got Bourbon Faced on Shit Street" T-shirts, or nearly matching "Drunk 1" and "Drunk 2" T-shirts. If you call out, "Roll Tide," to the zombie tourists, they have no will of their own and must respond in kind, "Roll Tide."

I offer the following opinion based on personal experience: If you don't believe in ghosts, live here a year and you will. I'm about as "normal" as they come. I grew up in Ohio, where *gosh darn* and *oh, nuts* were curse words. I am not prone to experience or believe in events that seem to be best classified as ghosts. What I have experienced here in New Orleans could logically be explained as a series of very isolated and repeated tectonic plate shifts. But the presence of ghosts is actually more plausible.

Why is New Orleans such a hotbed for hauntings and havoc?

Some feel it is our long history of death and disaster, including two fires that nearly destroyed the city (1788 and 1794), three outbreaks of yellow fever (1853, 1878, and 1905), and countless hurricanes and floods. Seasoned with an ample dose of voodoo and hoodoo, and simmered over our many aboveground cemeteries, and you have a recipe for a perfect woo-woo gumbo.

If you have even the slightest intuitive sense, you'll feel the seductive pull of psychic energy here. New Orleans has a vortex feeling that sucks in a certain type of person the same way Hilton Head draws in men who like to wear loud golf pants, or parts of Texas call to people who feel the need to build survivalist bunkers.

That you are now holding a book called *Fear Dat*, I assume you are among the susceptible to New Orleans' twisted charms. *Fear Dat* will, in part, provide a brief overview history of voodoo. It will trace vampirism back past Vlad the Impaler all the way to the ancient Egyptians. It will tell New Orleans' best ghost stories and most gruesome murders. But, like Mardi Gras and second line funerals, the point here is to participate. *Fear Dat* is aimed at visitors to New Orleans (or locals) who want to enrich their stay (or habitation) by doing something, not just reading about it. That might include getting the most reliable psychic reading, buying some authentic gris-gris from people who are really into voodoo, or finding the grave of Voo-doo Queen Marie Laveau or Ruthie the Duck Girl.

To quote our corrupt and now convicted ex-mayor Ray Nagin when he had his one shining moment, yelling at the Bush administration to wake up to the disaster that was Hurricane Katrina, "Get off your asses and let's do something!"

"Let's do something!"   RICK MOORE

FORE-WARNED

An Interview with a Bestselling Vampire Novelist

The dead walk alongside the living here and we talk to them all the time.

—Anne Rice

Anne Rice   <small>DAN NEWBURN</small>

Professor Longhair, Buddy Bolden, Dr. John, and Fats Domino all have their apostles, but Louis Armstrong is widely considered the King of New Orleans music. Blaze Starr beats out Evangeline the Oyster Girl as New Orleans' Queen of Burlesque. In the dark arts, Marie Laveau is unquestionably and literally the Queen of Voodoo.

Vampires, so much a pillar of the New Orleans community, can point directly to Anne Rice, the Queen of the Damned Best Sellers, as their resident regent. With her 13 vampire novels; 16 other novels about witches, werewolves, castratos, and Jesus as a seven-year-old; plus her 5 works of erotica written under pseudonyms, Anne has sold well over 100 million books, making her among the best-selling writers on the planet. Her writings have spawned 3 film adaptations, a mini-series, 10 comic books, and a short-lived Broadway play, *Lestat*, with music by Elton John.

She has also, more than anyone alive, revitalized the vampire mythology. She's actually revised vampires from monstrous loners like Dracula into the sympathetic characters like Louis de Pointe du Lac. Anne has said of her first book, "Vampires were these elegant, tragic, sensitive people. I was really just going with that feeling when writing *Interview with the Vampire*." Some Bram Stoker purists may cringe at the evolution from Dracula to these new "sensitive" vampires like Edward Cullen (*Twilight*) and Bill Compton (*True Blood*). They've become less monsters lurking in the shadows and more desirable boyfriend material. We here in New Orleans would never cringe. Anne's huge popularity has brought the city any number of economy-boosting film crews and countless tourists to drink in our vampire vibe.

She also brought us our resident saint, Brad Pitt. Before he bought a house in the Quarter, before he donated six million dollars of his own money to rebuild the Ninth Ward, before he demanded films like *12 Years a Slave*, *The Curious Case of Benjamin Button*, and *Killing Them Softly* be filmed in New Orleans, Brad came to New Orleans for the first time to make *Interview with the Vampire*. He told the *Times-Picayune*:

"I came to New Orleans back in 1994 doing the *Interview with the Vampire* movie, based on the Anne Rice novel, and fell in love with the city. It got under my skin. Everything was sexy and sultry. I'd ride my bike all over the place, amazed by the architecture. I'd return to New Orleans every chance I could. What can I say; it's got the best people, the best everything. It's the most interesting city in America."

Anne Rice also brought me to New Orleans. I first came here in May 1983 for the sole purpose of working with her. Like so many, I was immediately seduced by New Orleans unique charms and by day two, I knew I was home.

Therefore, it may be fitting that I begin *Fear Dat* with a quick interview Anne generously agreed to do during a time she was intensely putting the last touches on her new vampire novel, *Prince Lestat*.

Why do you feel New Orleans has become the epicenter for so many beautifully dark themes—voodoo, vampires, ghosts, psychic phenomena?

> *New Orleans is like a Caribbean colony, and the rise of voodoo in New Orleans has to do with the same elements that gave birth to it in the Caribbean islands—a mix of Catholicism and native religions. At least that's my conjecture. Why the city developed so many ghost stories, I don't know but I thrilled reading them as a child, and visiting the famous haunted houses in the Quarter and in other neighborhoods. Now, when it comes to fiction writers' using New Orleans as a setting for modern tales of vampires and ghosts and witches and such, well, it's the atmosphere and the ambience of the city—its Spanish colonial architecture, its antebellum Greek Revival houses, its dampness, its beauty, its cultural mix of Irish, Italian, Spanish, French, African, etc. The city's rich in ethnic customs, ethnic superstition, and legend and lore.*

What about New Orleans has most inspired or shaped your writing?

I grew up there and was always inspired by the physical beauty of the oaks, the flowers, and the architecture. I just loved it from the start. I loved the warmth and the ease of living in New Orleans, of walking and exploring. Just adored all of it. My heart stayed in New Orleans after I left and the longing for my beautiful home inspired much of my early writing, and inspires my writing now.

Is there a single chapter or paragraph you've created that you feel best captures the essence of New Orleans?

I can't point to one offhand but I suspect the writing in Interview with the Vampire *and in* The Witching Hour *might be my best on the topic of New Orleans. However,* The Feast of All Saints *was also a love letter to New Orleans by me.*

Have you had any personal experiences with ghosts, psychic events, or other phenomena that would be routinely dismissed by nonbelievers?

No, I've never had a single solitary supernatural experience in my entire life. Never seen a ghost, never felt anything paranormal. But wow, have I ever heard stories from my fellow New Orleanians on the ghosts they've seen and loved.

Now that you know what it means, what do you miss most about New Orleans?

I miss so much—the warm, flat streets, the giant oaks, the violet sky at evening, the humid and fragrant breeze, the scent of flowers, the marvelous colors of the old buildings in the Quarter, the spectacle of the river flowing at my feet, the sheer ease of roaming old neighborhoods where everywhere one looks, one finds a feast for the eyes, the easygoing happy people, so loving, so welcoming, so contented . . . I miss it painfully all the time. Someday I'll be back.

Quintessential second line

CHAPTER 1

Above-Ground Cemeteries, Second Lines, and Getting *the* Shaft

---

Dear America,
I suppose we should introduce ourselves: We're South Louisiana
. . . You probably already know that we talk funny and listen to
strange music and eat things you'd probably hire an exterminator
to get out of your yard. We dance even if there's no radio. We drink
at funerals. We talk too much and laugh too loud and live too
large and, frankly, we're suspicious of others who don't.
                        —**Chris Rose, bestselling author of** *One Dead in the Attic*

The past is not dead. In fact, it's not even past.   —**William Faulkner**

L et's begin at the beginning: Death.

Here in New Orleans, we may have hit upon a cure for cancer. Cancer is the #2 leading cause of death for the rest of America, but not here. We die before the cancer can get us. We lead the nation in kidney disease deaths, and we double as national champions for death from diabetes. Of course, given that our diet is built around deep-fried pork fat served with a side of bacon and a Sazerac and Abita chaser, these facts are not exactly shocking. As former *Times-Picayune* columnist Angus Lind wrote, "If you die of old age in New Orleans, it's your own damn fault." We're just different here.

The far and away strongest way we display our differences is what the still living do with the recently dearly departed. We haul 'em around town while drinking, dancing, waving our hankies, and carrying on. Then, we tuck them in little houses in our aboveground cemeteries (unless the little houses are full, in which case . . . no, I'll tell you about that later).

Mark Twain tagged our cemeteries with their lasting moniker when he wrote, "Our Cities of the Dead look just like our cities of the living—long narrow houses, housing multi-generations of the same family with above-ground basements." Twain always intended to live in his beloved New Orleans—he actually considered buying the house on First Street next door to what would later become Anne Rice's house—but he never was more than a visitor. He died in Redding, Connecticut. At the Old Brick Presbyterian Church in lower Manhattan, he probably had one of those boring old weepy funerals before being laid to rest (underground) at his wife's family plot in Elmira, New York. Knowing Mark Twain (which I don't) he probably would have much preferred a frenzied little second line in New Orleans than the dignified tribute he received in New York.

The commonly held view is that we bury the bodies aboveground because New Orleans is below sea level and if you bury your loved ones belowground, during a large storm with any flooding, the bodies will pop back up to the surface like rather unsightly Whack-a-Moles. This is only partly true. There are tales of early settlers' burying their neighbors and loved ones in the earthen levees and then, during heavy rains or floods, the decaying bodies of the dead would come swimming through the city streets. But since LaSalle first laid claim to New Orleans in 1682 and through the last of the 1700s, all burials in New Orleans were underground, 6 feet under being the standard.

Why 6 feet under? Most historians believe the practice of burying the dead 6 feet under started during London's Great Plague of 1665. As the disease spread, the mayor of London laid down the law, literally, about how to handle dead bodies infected with black plague, to avoid more infections and death. He created "Orders Conceived and Published by the Lord Major and Aldermen of the City of London, Concerning the Infection of the Plague," containing the phrase "all the graves shall be at least six feet deep." The belief was this was the proper depth to keep the plague-cooties away from the living.

Another far more juicy theory is that at 6 feet belowground, scavenging wolves and dogs would no longer be able to smell decaying bodies as blow-flies, rove beetles, and muscids eat their way from the inside to pierce the skin, releasing internal gases and beginning the process of turning the body into a stinky pool of liquefied organs. The strong odor of putrefaction brings around carnivores to start digging for tasty morsels of carcass.

The former Great Plague theory is probably more accurate, but I prefer the gruesomeness of the latter. And there's a phrase used in New Orleans (often): "Never let the truth get in the way of a good story."

The first public cemetery in New Orleans was erected on St. Peter Street in 1721. All burials there were in the ground, not above. Everything changed in 1788, but not because residents got tired of burying Grammy and Papaw over and over again each time they popped back up. 1788 was the year of the Great Fire, which burned down 80 percent of the city and killed over 1,200 people. The Saint Peter Street Cemetery couldn't handle the overflow of bodies, so they were taken outside the city walls and buried in the cypress swamp in what is now Basin Street between Conti and St. Louis Streets.

The original Saint Louis Cemetery was twice as big as it is today. Many resident dead in the original cemetery were dug up and relocated elsewhere when workers began digging the New Basin Canal right through the cemetery. The 1831 canal project intended to connect Lake Pontchartrain and the Mississippi River to form a shipping lane. An estimated 10,000 to 15,000 Irish immigrant workers died in the digging of the canal, most of them from yellow fever. Slaves were considered too valuable a commodity to risk working in the snake-filled, mosquito-laden marshes, but Irish immigrants flowing into America during the potato famine were a renewable resource. They worked for a dollar a day. If they keeled over, their bodies were simply tossed without markers in the recently turned-over muck and roadway fill.

The reason the St. Louis Cemetery is aboveground seems to be a jambalaya of economics, effective land use, the Catholic Church, and, as much as anything, a fashion statement. If you go to Paris or Barcelona, you'll find most of the cemeteries are likewise aboveground.

Toward the end of the 1700s, Paris experienced serious land shortages for burials. Bodies were shoved into the spaces in the sewers, and corpses *did* burst through walls at times of heavy rain. City planner Nicolas Frochot, a.k.a. the Father of Aboveground Cemeteries (though I may well be the only person in history to call him that) came up with the creative plan to deal with too many dead. He purchased land 2 miles outside the city of Paris for a new cemetery, named Père Lachaise. This was the first City of the Dead with aboveground mausoleums and tombs with space for multiple bodies in the same small "house." Its famous residents include Oscar Wilde, Colette, Isadora Duncan, Edith Piaf, Gertrude Stein, Marcel Proust, Marcel Marceau (but let's not talk about him), and the most visited grave site in Père Lachaise is Jim Morrison's. Like Parisian fashion or perfume, aboveground cemeteries spread as the "in" style of internment from Paris throughout France, then Spain and Portugal, and became a cultural tradition in areas colonized by France, Spain, and Portugal, New Orleans among them.

Then there's the Catholic Church, those fun folks who brought you the Inquisition, the Crusades, and witch hunts. They also held Galileo under house arrest the last nine years of his life, burned Joan of Arc at the stake, and tricked revisionist Czech priest Jan Hus to come hang out at the Vatican with the promise they'd do him no harm. They burned him at the stake, too.

There are those who believe the whole story of dead loved ones' popping up from New Orleans underground cemeteries was concocted, or at least greatly exaggerated, by the Catholic Church as a sales pitch, peddling fear and guilt to get parishioners to buy final resting places in the more expensive aboveground "houses" that were owned by, sold by, and fed the coffers of the Archdiocese of New Orleans.

The burial plots had their own set of house rules. They were large enough to hold more than a single body. But, by law, you got cut off after burying two fresh ones. Once occupied, the burial houses were sealed, and had to remain sealed, for 366 days. It is believed 366 days, or a year and a day, was decreed when New Orleans was hit with outbreaks of yellow fever. The living (incorrectly) worried they could catch the disease from the dead bodies.

The other advantage of the year-and-a-day rule is the dead body would pass through a New Orleans summer inside the vault. The Catholic Church did not allow cremation. When it's 110 degrees outside on an oppressively hot August day in New Orleans, it'll be well above 300 degrees inside the tomb. The body would be cooked and naturally cremated. At the end of the 366 days, the vault could be opened, and the ashes and what was left of bone could be scooped and bagged, then placed at the base of the tomb to make space for the next fresh body.

If members of your family died during the 366 days, they were out of luck. They weren't getting in. Each cemetery is lined with oven walls, a great number of internment spots that look very much like brick pizza ovens.

These are rental properties for when a third family member passes away while the tomb is still sealed. A family can store a dearly departed there until the 366 days are up, the family tomb reopened, cremated residents scooped and bagged, making room for the more recently dead to be moved over from the oven wall.

If you failed to pay the oven rent, the same thing would happen to the stored body as would a living body for failure to pay rent. It would be evicted. A cemetery employee would use a long pole to push the body to the back of the "oven," where an opening in the floor would allow the remains to drop through a shaft to the bottom of the vault and mix with the ashes or jawbones of other nonpaying deadbeats. This practice is the derivation of the phrases *getting the shaft* or *being shafted*. Use of the long shaft may also be the derivation of the phrase not touching something *with a 10-foot pole*.

The 1853 outbreak of yellow fever claimed 7,849 residents of New Orleans. The press and the medical profession did not alert residents of the outbreak until more than one thousand people died because the New Orleans business community pressured silence. They feared any word of an epidemic would cause a quarantine to be placed on the city and that their trade business would suffer. However, in a city of only 154,000 people, when nearly 8,000 residents drop dead with yellowed skin, vomiting black gruel, and bleeding from the nose, mouth, and eyes, eventually locals started noticing.

Reports from the period describe long lines of carriages and wagons in traffic jams, streaming from New Orleans to the Cities of the Dead, carrying the overwhelming number of victims to their graves. Funerals had been banned at St. Louis Cathedral because of fear of infection. The Catholic Church built a little chapel on Rampart Street, now known as Our Lady of Guadalupe, so that yellow fever victims could be blessed before they were hastily buried. The sheer mass of corpses often demanded quick and shallow burials.

The *New Orleans Daily Crescent* newspaper reported:

> At the gates, the winds brought intimation of the corruption lurking within. Not a puff was not laden with the rank atmosphere from rotting corpses. Inside they were piles by the fifties, exposed to the heat of the sun, swollen with corruption, bursting their coffin lids what a feast of horrors. Inside, corpses piled in pyramids and without the gates, old and withered crones and

fat huxter women dispensing ice creams and confections, and brushing away the green bottleflies that hovered on their merchandise and that anon buzzed away to drink dainty inhalations from the green and festering corpses.

Sounds a little like a description of the current Southern Decadence Festival, held in New Orleans each September.

New Orleans being New Orleans, and committed to the philosophy "anything worth doing is worth overdoing," now takes 21st-century preparation of dead bodies to the next level, pushing the envelope, literally, out of the box.

When beloved musician Uncle Lionel Batiste died in 2012, the hundreds of people attending his funeral received a surprise greeting. Said one attendee, "They've even got his watch on the mannequin's hand," referring to the lifelike figure standing in the funeral home's chapel. But it wasn't a mannequin, noted another. "That's him."

Several of Mr. Batiste's children, in consultation with Louis Charbonnet, owner of Charbonnet-Labat-Glapion Funeral Home, concocted the idea of standing him up for his wake. During his 50 years in the funeral business, Charbonnet had never before embalmed a body in a lifelike pose. The deceased Mr. Batiste was presented standing up against a faux street lamp, decked out in his signature man-about-town finery. Uncle Lionel's body, in his habitual-in-life sunglasses, wore a cream-colored suit, tasseled loafers, an ornate necktie with matching pocket square, and a bowler hat. His bass drum and his Treme Brass Band uniform were positioned nearby. His hands rested atop his omnipresent cane. The gold watch draped across his left palm rather than on his wrist was his trademark, representing his desire to always have "time on my hands." "That's something I've never seen before," said Charbonnet, "It's perfect. It's a wonderful, strange thing."

Not quite two years later, philanthropist, socialite, and legendary party hostess Mickey Easterling went out in the larger-than-life, in this case larger-than-death, fashion in which she lived. More than a thousand people attended her memorial service at the Saenger Theater. Mickey was presented casually perched on a wrought-iron garden bench. To her right, on a small table, sat a bottle of her favorite champagne, Veuve Clicquot, and in

Second line for Lionel Batiste in the Treme   DEREK BRIDGES / CREATIVE COMMONS

her right hand was a Waterford crystal champagne flute she used to carry around when restaurant glassware just wouldn't do. Mickey was dressed in her famous accoutrements: a Leonardo outfit, large floral hat, feather boa, and cigarette holder. Her dead body wore a diamond-studded pin, spelling out "B-I-T-C-H" on her chest.

In June 2014, diorama funerals crossed over from noted musicians and socialites to mainstream, everyday people when Miriam "Mae-Mae" Burbank was given the Charbonnet Funeral Home treatment. She was memorialized with a "last party." At the funeral, Burbank was sitting at a fold-up table, wearing a Saints jersey, holding a menthol cigarette and a can of beer. A crossword puzzle and toy Saints helmets were resting on the table.

Long before this new trend in funerals, New Orleans had an earlier style by which grave sites had a large number of multiple residents thematically grouped. Funeral monuments were dedicated to an association or group rather than identified by an individual or a family. Many poor immigrants could not afford funeral expenses or a personal tomb. Benevolent societies were formed in New Orleans, allowing members to pool their financial resources and build "society vaults" in the city's established cemeteries.

In St. Louis Cemetery #1, Marie Laveau, Ernest Morial, and Homer Plessy share the grounds with the tallest monument in the cemetery, the Italian Mutual Benevolent Society tomb. The Italian tomb has space for more than a thousand remains. Most famously it was used as the background in the LSD scene from *Easy Rider*, where Peter Fonda climbed all over the monument and Dennis Hopper allegedly tore the head off the *Charity* statue.

At the end of Canal Street, where New Orleans meets Metairie, are the Cypress Grove and Greenwood Cemeteries, both built by the Firemen's Charitable and Benevolent Association. The FCBA was founded in 1834 to help arrange burials as well as take care of the families when nearly impoverished all-volunteer firemen lost their lives in the line of duty. There's also a Police Mutual Benevolent Association, a Confederate monument, and the Benevolent and Protective Order of Elks, Lodge 30.

Whereas most of the societies helped bury European immigrants or people employed in professions predominantly occupied by whites, the tradition of trade or ethnic group burial sites actually has roots in Africa. In Benin and Nigeria of western Africa, the secret societies of the Dahomeans and Yorubans were created to assure fellow tribesmen that a proper burial would be performed upon their death.

While benevolent associations are a funeral rite of the past and the diorama presentations of Uncle Lionel and Miss Mickey may or may not be a future trend, the tradition of second line jazz funerals is a constant, bridging the past and the present.

Second line processions have been called the "quintessential New Orleans art form." Once again, the origins come from West Africa. During a traditional African circle dance, adults formed the inner circle and children assembled on the periphery. In the New Orleans style, the family of the

Memorial for Destitute Boys

KAREN SCHECHNER

deceased forms the first line. The second line are friends and more distant relatives, with plenty of room for people who didn't even know the deceased but want to join the party.

Brass bands accompany funeral party from church to grave site, playing traditional slow spiritual dirges and hymns like "Just a Closer Walk with Thee" and "Amazing Grace." Leaving the cemetery, however, becomes a completely different tune. Handkerchiefs carried for sobbing and grief become a sashaying flag. Umbrellas used as protection from intense sun or rain become a festively twirling joystick. The music kicks up to New Orleans style. "Some people call it funk," notes Big Chief Jake Millon in a 1976 documentary *The Black Indians of New Orleans*, "but to us it's strictly second line." Classic songs for the second line leaving the cemetery, or what's been called " a jazz funeral without a body," include "Hey Pocky-a-Way," the 1960s

Mandy Walker

I don't know about you, but when I hear the job title "director of Save Our Cemeteries," I envision a schoolmarmish 50-something who spends her days leafing through yellowed archives of old obituary notices. Mandy Walker, the real-life director, looks more like the director of the New Orleans Film Festival, or one of the New Orleans Nightingales, exceptionally cool female singers like Ingrid Lucia, Meschiya Lake, and Debbie Davis.

Save Our Cemeteries, a nonprofit group, was established in 1974 to preserve and protect our cemeteries. Its first act was to save the oven wall vaults alongside St. Louis #2 when the Catholic Archdiocese was considering tearing it down and replacing the wall with a chain-link fence.

Currently, Save Our Cemeteries has five hundred volunteers and eight hundred members, but Mandy is the only full-time employee, joined by four part-time workers for the day-to-day administration. The organization's annual budget is around $200,000. Small in size, it is immeasurable in its importance to the preservation of New Orleans' unique but twisted character. On business cards and flyers, its tag line reads, "Tomb It May Concern."

SOC offers authentic and historically accurate cemetery tours. It also hosts four main fund-raising events, including A Run Through History, a 5K race through the Metairie Cemetery, making it the largest cemetery road race in the nation; Cemeteryscape, an international cemetery photography competition and exhibit; a cocktail gala; and a day-long cemetery seminar and educational symposium. All of the proceeds from these events benefit the restoration, education, and advocacy efforts of SOC. It's also actively involved in cemetery cleanups, cemetery security, community outreach, educational programs and tomb restoration—such as SOC's recent cleanup (and at great cost) of a Day-Glo pink assault on Marie Laveau's tomb. Its focus is on tombs that are deemed abandoned, ones that have not seen a new burial in 50 or more years and have no known descendants or owners. Families are responsible for their tombs if heirs or future residents are still alive and kicking.

Mandy Walker got her job with Save Our Cemeteries through a posting on Craig's List, or the same way pet sitters and pizza delivery people get theirs. SOC was looking for a part-time membership coordinator. She'd never even heard of the organization but was immediately interested in the job. Her mother had grown up in New Orleans. Whenever the family visited, they'd drive all over the city just to look at houses, drinking in the city's unique architecture and history. The cemeteries hit on both notes of her interests. The Cities of the Dead are architecturally magnificent

Mandy Walker

and an essential pillar of our history. As she notes, "The stories of the people that are interred inside of them never cease to amaze me. The cemeteries here are just fascinating and can tell us so much about the history of this beautiful old city and the people who built it."

Mandy started working part-time in March 2008. She began taking on more responsibilities and was eventually hired as a full-time employee. When the most recent director stepped down, she figured, "What the hell, I'll apply for the position. I've got nothing to lose!" She'd been with the organization for six years and had a master's degree in nonprofit management for the arts, so it wasn't like she didn't have the grave cred to land the job. As of June 1, 2014, she became the new director for Save Our Cemeteries.

Mandy views her top priority is to get locals to care as much about the cemeteries as the waves of tourists do: "To get locals back in to care for their family tombs. So many cemeteries are part of residential neighborhoods that they sometimes get overlooked and therefore, neglected. This leads to theft, vandalism, and the tombs' falling apart without proper, ongoing maintenance. We want people to care about what happens to their neighborhood cemeteries. It's good for the city as a whole, fights blight, and pays homage the 'dearly departed.' Our cemeteries are so very unique here and yet they are taken for granted by some."

She and the small staff of part-timers and mostly volunteers, she describes as close-knit. "We are all extremely passionate about the work that we do. We are like a family here." Her personal favorite cemeteries are Odd Fellow's Rest and St. Louis Cemetery #2 for a variety of reasons, mainly because of the ornate ironwork in these two cemeteries.

I asked her if she had any cool, creepy, or humorous anecdotes about something she directly experienced in the cemeteries. Mandy replied, "I've seen exposed remains, unfortunately, and the contents of caskets strewn about. (A deceased woman's wig and teeth, to be exact.) I also saw inside of a tomb that was broken into. It contained the most beautiful antebellum iron casket I have ever seen, and it was in excellent condition. It was clear that someone was coming back for it later, for God knows what reason. It was very disturbing to me. I'll never forget that particular visit."

Over the years, she's also been alerted to evidence that living people have taken up residence in the cemeteries. A few years back, a spice rack, complete with spices, was found in Lafayette Cemetery #1. I forgot to ask her if the spice bottles were opened. But when delivered pizza boxes were also discovered in the same spot, evidence pointed to a squatter rather than pizza-eating ghost.

To help the cause, you can take a tour, make a donation, or become a member. You can do all three on the website, www.saveourcemeteries.org, or by writing to soc@saveourcemeteries.org.

Or, you can take the Funeral Urn Challenge. You can post a video on social media, showing yourself dumping a bucket of cremated ashes over your head, or just donate $100.

(Note: The Funeral Urn Challenge is not a real fund-raising event. But it should be.)

Dixie Cups hit "Jock-a-Mo," and the newish (1990s) but seemingly timeless anthem of Rebirth Brass Band, "Do Whatcha Wanna."

It's basically a frenzied celebration for the life that was.

African music and burial traditions took hold in New Orleans largely because the French and then Spanish who controlled the city granted more autonomy to the slaves than did transplanted uptight Protestants from England who spread their pasty styles over the rest of the country (houses should be white; clothing can mix black and white; music should be respectful in tone). The French and Spanish allowed former Africans to keep their traditions and express their music and dance heritage every Sunday, the slaves' one day free from work, in Congo Square.

Historically, second lines occurred in predominantly African American neighborhoods of Treme and Central City. But today, they can be pretty much seen all over the city, and not just for funerals. There are second lines staged for weddings, sometimes a store opening, and cutting through the Fairgrounds during Jazz Fest.

It may be just me, but I pretty much despise fake second line parades, hired out by event planners so conventioneers from Cleveland can stiffly shuffle from their hotel lobby out to Canal Street, waving hankies like they're having a stroke and trying to hail an EMS vehicle. (I probably just lost 390,000 potential buyers from Cleveland, but having grown up there, hopefully I can get away with insulting my old hometown the way only you can make fun of your family but outsiders cannot.) There's something very Vanilla Ice or Milli Vanilli, about the whole concocted-for-tourists second line thing.

While standing behind a concierge desk, I have been asked any number of times, "Where can we see a second line parade?" as though the answer was as simple as telling them where to eat a beignet or drink a hurricane. My pat answer has been, "Well, someone needs to die first. Preferably a noted musician." I get a lot of blank stares from that one.

CHAPTER 2

A Bone Watcher's
Field Guide to New Orleans

The first thing you notice about New Orleans are the burying grounds—the cemeteries—and they're a cold proposition. Greek, Roman, sepulchres, palatial mausoleums made to order, phantomesque, signs and symbols of hidden decay. The past doesn't pass away so quickly here. —**Bob Dylan**

I wish to be cremated. One tenth of my ashes shall be given to my agent, as written in our contract. —**Groucho Marx**

There are 38 cemeteries in New Orleans. If you are visiting the city, you just have to face the fact that you aren't going to get to them all in one trip—unless you approach vacations like my dad. My dad, and I think all dads of that era, measured the success of a vacation by how many miles you packed into each day. On a trip out West, we drove by (but did not stop at) the Corn Palace, Wall Drug, and the (disputed) World's Largest Ball of Twine in Cawker City, Kansas. I think my dad said all three roadside attractions were "on the wrong side of the road" as we zipped by.

This chapter will focus on just a few of the cemeteries most popular with tourists. Think about that last sentence for a moment. In what other city are graveyard visits high on the must-do list for visiting tourists? When traveling to Miami, is there much of an impulse to go to Flagler Memorial Park? Does the Masonic cemetery in San Francisco share equal billing with the Golden Gate Bridge, Chinatown, and Fisherman's Wharf?

For some visiting tourist, this chapter may be the most valued in the book. It will map out who's buried where, so you can stroll up to Professor Longhair's vault or Marie Laveau's tomb to pay homage or to ask for favors from the other side. With apologies to Étienne de Boré, New Orleans' first

St. Louis Cemetery

FEAR DAT

mayor, ragtime composer Paul Sarebresole, and the entire Musson family, page count prohibits me from including all deserving of mention.

St. Louis Cemetery #1

LOCATION: 501 Basin St. (between Conti and St. Louis Sts.)
HOURS: 9:00 A.M.–3:00 P.M. Mon–Sat; 9:00 A.M. –12:00 P.M. Sun

Effective March 1, 2015, the Archdiocese of New Orleans closed this cemetery to free access. You now can only enter with an approved tour guide, which requires you to pay between $20 and $25, and the tour guide pays the Archdiocese over $4,000 a year to be in their approved list. I personally find this wildly offensive and a money-grab by the Archdiocese. The cemetery is an essential piece of our history and should be as accessible as the Alamo in San Antonio or the Liberty Bell in Philadelphia. However, my letters to the mayor and head of the Catholic Church and signing a petition and staging a protest in the cemetery did nothing to block the action. Hopefully, it will be repealed by the time you visit.

St. Louis's residents of the oldest and most visited aboveground cemetery in New Orleans include Marie Laveau, our Voodoo Queen, and it is the future home of Nicolas Cage, our Scenery Chewing King. There are a number of society tombs: for Société Française, the benevolent society of France; another for the Portuguese Benevolent Association; one for the Orleans Battalion of Artillery, dedicated to anonymous soldiers killed at the Battle of New Orleans and which uses once active cannons as a hedge around the monument; and, most famously, the Cervantes Mutual Benefit Society or Italian Mutual Benevolent Society.

The following are some of the most distinguished stiffs to call this place their (permanent) home:.

 Marie Laveau is believed to be buried here. Some think the grave actually holds her daughter, also named Marie Laveau. Others think they're both buried there. There are stories that her bones were removed by voodoo practitioners to be used as high-octane gris-gris, or that her body was tossed into Lake Pontchartrain for reasons unclear. Regardless of what may or may not be the case, this is the second-most-visited grave site in America. Elvis's in Memphis is number one. The vault is covered in three X's, representing "spirit, unity, and power" in the voodoo tradition. The theory is if you scribble three X's, knock three times, turn around three times, or spit spirits (the alcoholic kind) from your mouth onto the grave three times, your wish will be granted. The Save Our Cemeteries association asks if you must write three X's, please use chalk and not a permanent ink marker.

You'll also notice a variety of offerings at the base of the grave: fake flowers, loose change, Mardi Gras beads, a pen out of ink, a number of lipstick tubes, rosary medals, an unused condom pack—pretty much anything. The point is, when you visit Marie Laveau's grave, you should honor the sacred spot and leave her something. If you choose to hoard your stuff and leave her nothing, don't blame me when you go home and your teeth start falling out. You were warned.

The tomb of Marie Laveau

There have been sightings of a large black snake nearby the tomb. It's alleged to be the ghost of Zombi, Marie Laveau's snake. A large black snake alone is enough to give me the willies. Having it be the ghost of a snake seems to be gilding the lily.

At the tail end of 2013, some brave but twisted soul jumped the cemetery wall at night and painted Marie's famous vault with pink latex paint. Latex paint, which does not breathe and traps in moisture, can ruin brick-and-mortar tombs. It required months of work and over $10,000 to repair. Of course, we're guessing this was nothing compared to the *Game of Thrones*–style vengeance the painter-perpetrator has endured at the hands of Marie. A quick Google search of the most horrific recent deaths includes that a man choked to death in a cockroach-eating contest and another man suffocated in massive amounts of elephant shit (both of these are real causes of death). I'm guessing one of them was the person who dared to desecrate Marie Laveau's tomb.

⚜ Right next to Marie was New Orleans' first black mayor and civil rights activist Ernest "Dutch" Morial. He was also the first African American to graduate from LSU, the first African American assistant to the US Attorney's Office, and the first elected to the Louisiana Legislature since Reconstruction. The Morials are sort of the Kennedys or Roosevelts of New Orleans. Ernest and Sybil had five children. His son Marc served eight years as New Orleans second black mayor and now serves as president of the National Urban League. His daughter Monique was elected a City Court judge. Cheri became the chairwoman of the Baton Rouge Downtown Development District. Jacques became a political consultant, and Julie became a doctor. Dutch was a combative and combustible politician, called everything from "feisty" to "uppity," depending on who was doing the calling. Noted a close friend, "Dutch wouldn't bend his knee to anyone." UNO professor Arnold Hirsch said of Morial, "He had his signature on almost every case that began to dismantle the edifice of Jim Crow here, brick by brick." He's also the namesake for New Orleans' Convention Center, which conventioneers seem unable to pronounce. It's "MORE-ee-ALL." The tomb still honors the mayor, but his body was recently moved to St. Louis #2.

⚜ Paul Morphy was a precursor for Bobby Fischer. In his day, he was the far and away greatest chess player in the world and an equally far and away loony loner. Morphy became international chess champion at age 19 but grew bored traveling Europe and Russia and easily winning every match. He returned to New Orleans in 1859 and officially retired from chess at age 23. Paul's plans were to become a lawyer, but instead he lounged for years, alone in idle wealth inside his family's home at 417 Royal Street, or what would become the location for Brennan's famous (pink) restaurant. Morphy was found dead in his bathtub at age 43. The official cause of death was cardiac arrest, presumably from jumping into a cold bath on a particularly hot day. The "official" report made no mention of the collection of ladies' shoes that encircled his tub o' death.

There is no name attached to one bright, white, obviously newish pyramid-shaped tomb near the Conti Street entrance, just the words *Omnia Ab Uno*. The translation is "All from one." There are also lipstick kisses on the edifice, just like the three X's on Marie Laveau's. The kisses were not left to grant wishes, but to honor the owner and eventual resident, Nicolas Cage. His is one of several Egyptian pyramid tombstones in our cemeteries. All things Egyptian were popular in America during the first half of the 19th century. The craze was sparked by the uncovering of Tutankhamen's tomb in 1922, which spread everywhere in newsreel footage and magazine covers. Eventually it bled into newly popular architectural styles. The all-seeing eye above the pyramid was added to the US dollar bill during this time.

 Italian Mutual Benevolent Society's is the tallest monument in the cemetery—14 feet 6 inches high—and has room for more than a thousand remains. Many call it the *Easy Rider* tomb because in the movie starring Peter Fonda and Dennis Hopper, they pick up two prostitutes and bring them to the cemetery, where all four take LSD. Fonda then climbs up this tomb to have a chat with the statue. Hopper remains below with the prostitutes doing what one does with prostitutes. The Catholic Archdiocese was not tickled pink when it viewed the final film and since then has instituted very tight guidelines before it grants permission to any film company.

Duparc Locoul is the family tomb for the owners of the often visited Laura Plantation. Nearby Oak Alley is the #1 most visited plantation on the planet. You have seen it. Oak Alley has been the set of countless movies and Beyoncé videos. Both plantations are about an hour and 15 minutes outside New Orleans. I consider the Laura Plantation the more interesting, as it was run by four generations of women. Under Napoleonic Code, women could own property, run businesses, and vote from the 1700s on, not 1920 like the rest of America. The plantation matriarchs kept willing it to their daughters because they thought their sons were idiots. There are also three of the original 69 slave quarters still intact on the property. Under *coartación*, a policy introduced by the Spanish, slavery was also quite different in New Orleans. Slaves could buy their freedom here, unlike anywhere else in the nation. In a questionable pursuit of more tourist dollars, Oak Alley is building new slave quarters to offer as part of their visits.

 Homer Plessy was Rosa Parks more than 50 years before Rosa Parks. Homer was $\frac{1}{8}$ black, making him black in the eyes of the law, but he could easily pass for white. He purposefully sat in the whites-only car of a railroad train with the full intention of being arrested. Plessy was a member of the Comité des Citoyens, or Citizens' Committee of New Orleans, formed to strike down segregation laws. Contrary to the rest of the country, blacks in New Orleans, even before the Civil War, were mostly already "free men of color" by being born Creole, were runaway "maroons," or had bought their freedom under *coartación*. In New Orleans, former slaves lost rights rather than gained freedom after the Civil War. Plessy took his case all the way to the US Supreme Court. On May 18, 1896, the court issued its infamous "separate-but-equal" ruling that basically legalized segregation anywhere in America, better known as Jim Crow.

 Bernard Xavier Philippe de Marigny de Mandeville was the wealthiest teenager in the world when both his parents died. Displaying all the reserve and self-control of most 15-year-old boys, he blew his fortune traveling Europe and playing (and losing at) the dice game crapaud, which today we shorten to *craps*. Other than flushing his seven-million-dollar inheritance (this was seven million 19th-century dollars, making him a 15-year-old billionaire by today's standards), Bernie's greatest accomplishment was introducing the game of craps to America. In order to pay off his gambling debts, he sold much of his plantation to New Orleans in what is now the Marigny and Bywater neighborhoods. Again displaying his youth, Bernie christened the streets running through his property with all the solemn thoughtfulness of teenagers naming their garage bands. After acquiring his land, the city changed many of his names under Ordinance Number 395. Fortunately Desire Street, Peace, Frenchman, Piety, and Pleasure remain today, but Love Street became Rampart. Also, Crap Street has been changed to St. Claude after a church petitioned the city because it didn't want to be known as "the Church on Crap."

The Protestant Section is where the Catholic Archdiocese corralled all the non-Catholic corpses. After the Louisiana Purchase, Puritan Americans flooded into the city to live and, eventually, they would need a place to be buried. That place was the low-rent section of St. Louis #1, where the infidel bodies were shoved—unadorned, without vaults—at the far back left corner of the cemetery. Even this wasn't the final resting place for most of them as the city expanded outside the French Quarter and projects like the Basin Street Canal pressed at the borders of the cemetery. Many bodily remains may have been lost when Protestant graves were moved to First Protestant Cemetery on Girod Street in 1822. When the Girod Street Cemetery was deconsecrated in 1957, most white corpses were moved to the Holt Cemetery and most blacks were shipped to Providence Memorial Park. The Superdome stands atop these old burial grounds. Some long-suffering football fans felt those first 43 years of terrible "Aints" teams were caused by playing on cursed or haunted burial grounds. Even today, if you dig a swimming pool in the French Quarter or the CBD (City Business District) sections of town, as Vincent Marcello did in 2010, you're likely to find some buried bodies. Vincent found 15 caskets.

Clarisse Duralde Claiborne was the second wife of Louisiana's first governor after the US purchase in 1803. William C. C. Claiborne was sent down to rule over the new territory and was immediately unpopular with the French residents. For one, he didn't speak a word of their language. He quickly followed up with the gaff of placing a $500 bounty on the pirate Jean Lafitte. Lafitte was no swashbuckling pirate, more like a Tony Soprano mob boss. He was beloved in the city for providing Walmart prices on goods stolen off ships in the Gulf. They loved him even more when Lafitte laughed off Claiborne's bounty by posting his own, $5,000 for the governor.

Following the death of Claiborne's first (American) wife, many felt he chose the French Creole Clarisse Duralde as his second wife to soften his image. It probably worked just as well as Michael "Tough Guy" Dukakis's riding a tank or George Herbert Walker "Just Folks" Bush's trying to navigate a supermarket. After only two years of marriage, Clarisse passed away. When Claiborne died, his body was not permitted to be buried next to his wife because, unlike her, he was not a Catholic.

There is a Claiborne family vault in the Metairie Cemetery. His remains might have been moved there, or they might be mixed in with those of the transients Protestants on Girod Street, or he may still be hanging out, just out of reach of Clarisse, in St. Louis #1.

 Benjamin Latrobe has been called "the Father of American Architecture." He is most famous for designing the Capitol Building in Washington, DC. In New Orleans, he lived long enough to complete the new central tower of the St. Louis Cathedral and the whole of the US Customs House before he succumbed to yellow fever.

The Customs House has the same facade on all four sides because, when it was built, the architects weren't sure which would be the main thoroughfare, Canal Street or Decatur or Chartres, and they wanted to make a nice first impression. Today the building houses the Insectarium, the largest bug museum in America and in whose snack bar you can dine on (what I hear) are the tastiest bugs anywhere.

Years before Latrobe, the original designer of the original St. Louis Cathedral, which burned, was French engineer Adrien de Pauger. Pauger requested to be buried under the floorboards of the church as this was considered an honor. One hundred thirty-some popes are buried under the floor of St. Peter's Basilica. Unfortunately, he died in 1726, before the church was completed. As an ad hoc measure, to honor his wishes, workers tossed Pauger's body in a wall and just kept going.

 The Barbarin family has deep musical roots in New Orleans, dating back to the 1800s, when patriarch Isidore Barbarin played alto horn and mellophone in the Excelsior Brass Band. The Barbarin musical tradition carries on to this day: jazz trombonist Lucien Barbarin has played with Wynton Marsalis and Harry Connick Jr.

Paul Barbarin died in 1969 while leading a brass band in a Mardi Gras parade. Nephew and namesake (and still alive) Paul Barbarin heard about Hazel, wife of Lloyd Washington of the Ink Spots, having no money to bury her husband. In a room at the Mother-in-Law Lounge, Barbarin signed documents to grant use of his family's tomb to local musicians.

"People just want to do something for musicians who have done so much for this city," Paul said. Six of the 18 vaults in the 20-foot-high

Barbarin family tomb will always be reserved for musicians. Lloyd Washington was the first to be buried there, on October 23, 2004.

To add to the pleasure of your cemetery stroll, St. Louis #1 is also supposed to be haunted. A ghost named Alphonse has taken the hand of visitors, telling them his name and asking if they can help him find his way home. A second ghost, Henry, had his burial site sold while he was at sea and upon his return, his dead body was dumped in a potter's field. His ghost is alleged to wander the cemetery where he wished to be buried. Henry sometimes approaches visitors, always in a courteous way. He asks is they can help him locate the Vignes tomb. When a new burial is taking place, Henry's been known to butt in and inquire if he can squeeze in and join the deceased in their vault.

St. Louis Cemetery #2

LOCATION: Claiborne Ave. (between St. Louis and Iberville Sts.)
Entrance gates at Bienville and Conti Sts.
HOURS: 9:00 A.M.–3:00 P.M. Mon–Sat; Sunday: 9:00 A.M.–12:00 P.M. Sun

St. Louis #2 is, quite frankly, not a cemetery where I would choose to wander. That's because many others choose not to wander there; it has become a human version of a cat colony. Homeless, addicted, or mentally unstable persons often tend to huddle here between the tombstones or draped across slabs of concrete. But around these unsavory loiterers, there's a lot of history.

In 1823, the City Council opened this new cemetery farther removed from city residents, based on the erroneous belief that yellow fever– and cholera-infested bodies could spread the disease by miasmas.

Most important, St. Louis Cemetery #2 led to the creation of the Save Our Cemeteries organization. In 1974, the Archdiocese of New Orleans proposed to tear down the wall vaults and replace them with a chain-link fence. Preservationists in the city were appalled, and SOC was founded in response. Over the next 10 years, working with the Archdiocese, the City, the local mason's union, and other preservation organizations, SOC was able to restore the wall vaults rather than destroy them.

Buried in St. Louis #2 are the pirate Dominique You, who was a lieutenant in the Gulf of Mexico's largest pirate operation and said to be Jean

Lafitte's brother; New Orleans mayor Nicholas Girod, who famously offered his home to Napoleon Bonaparte to come live in exile; and Jacques Phillippe Villeré, Louisiana's first native-born governor. There are keynote musicians, like Danny Barker, Earl King, and Ernie K-Doe, buried in a family vault dedicated to musicians, much like the Barbarin tomb in St. Louis #1. Ernie K-Doe, who first named himself "Mister M-Nauga-Ma-Hyde" and later began billing himself as "the Emperor of the Universe," was supposed to be buried in his family's plot outside the city. But his wife, Antoinette, stepped in: "If you're from New Orleans, you want to be buried in New Orleans."

If she ever gets voted in for sainthood (and she's been close) Henriette Delille will become the cemetery's most noteworthy resident. So far, she's made it all the way up to "venerable," which is kind of like being a brown belt in karate. Henriette was a descendant of slaves and founded the first black religious community, Sisters of the Holy Family. The fact that a black woman is even being considered for sainthood by white men in robes, I think, should count as one of her miracles.

Save Our Cemeteries does offer tours of St. Louis #2, but only twice per year. You can call (504) 525-3377 if you are interested in checking on the next available tour.

St. Louis Cemetery #3

LOCATION: 3421 Esplanade Ave. (near City Park)
HOURS: 9:00 A.M.–3:00 P.M. Mon–Sat; 9:00 A.M.–12:00 P.M. Sun

When the city needed more space to bury the overflow of bodies from an outbreak of yellow fever in 1848, this tract of land was bought from Felix Labatut for $15,000. Previously, it had been a leper colony with a small makeshift burial ground known as Bayou Cemetery.

The original St. Louis #3 cemetery was expanded in 1865 and again in the 1980s. There are now approximately 10,000 burial sites, which include 5,000 mausoleums, 3,000 wall vaults, 2,000 individual family tombs, and 12 society tombs. This cemetery is larger than both St. Louis #1 and #2 put together.

Because of its easy access (just pull over and park on Esplanade), St. Louis #3 is used by the majority of city tour companies. It is an active cemetery grounds with a waiting list for plots nearly as long as the one for Saints season tickets.

St. Louis #3 is also a hot spot to bury the professionally religious, with several tombs for different orders of nuns and priests. There is a tomb for the Little Sisters of the Poor on St. Peter aisle. A statue of Mother Teresa greets you inside the front gate.

There's also "Chef's Corner," adjacent family tombs of New Orleans' leading restaurant families of Tujague, Prudhomme, and Galatoire.

E. J. Bellocq is buried here. He'd been a weird loner who bounced from a variety of jobs as bookkeeper and clerk for various businesses. His mother's death seemed to release Bellocq to quit his dull jobs and become something of a French Quarter dandy, clad in flamboyant scarves and monogrammed jewelry, and able to pursue his true love as a photographer. He made his new reputation photographing buildings, ships, and landmarks throughout the city, but posthumously he is now most famous for his peculiar private personal collection. He died in 1949 of, well, pretty much everything (cerebral arteriosclerosis, diabetes, obesity, a concussion, senility, and old age). Entering his musty apartment after his death, family found it strewn with collapsed furniture, broken lamps, and dismembered pieces of photographic equipment.

They also discovered Bellocq's collection of picture after picture he'd taken of the prostitutes of New Orleans' Storyville. Some subjects were partially clothed, others naked except for the black masks they wore, and, most bizarrely, many of the images were intentionally damaged. The faces of the prostitutes had been scratched out. Some believe Bellocq's Jesuit priest brother did it; it would be fitting for a Jesuit to hide the face but leave images of breasts and vaginas untouched. Others think E. J. himself is the most likely candidate, since the damage seems to have been done while the emulsion was still wet. We'll never know if the scratch-outs were done to (a) protect the identity of the women photographed, (b) make the images somehow more erotic or accessible to the socially stilted photographer, or (c) this is some kind of artistic statement.

The most noteworthy grave is not really a grave, but rather a bodiless monument to James Gallier. His real body was lost at sea when the paddle steamer *Evening Star* sank in a hurricane. Born James Gallagher in County Louth, Ireland, he worked in England until he went bankrupt and immigrated to America to start over.

One of the "Storyville" prostitutes photographed by E. J. Bellocq—with her face still intact.

Lafayette Cemetery   Rob Webster

In the mid-19th century, James (now) Gallier was one of the most prominent architects of New Orleans. Many of the city's most historic and renowned buildings, including National Historic Landmarks Gallier Hall, the former City Hall, and the Pontalba Buildings that line Jackson Square, are his designs. Today, you can tour his personal home at 1132 Royal Street. The Gallier House, like his buildings, displayed the latest in developments in design, in this case, indoor plumbing

None of his success in New Orleans would have been possible had Gallagher not heeded the advice of a friend back in New York. Before he moved to New Orleans, he was told, "If you expect to do any business there, you'd better have a French name."

Lafayette Cemetery #1

LOCATION: 1400 Washington Ave. (between Prytania and Coliseum Sts.)
HOURS: 7:00 A.M.–2:30 P.M. Mon–Fri; 7:00 A.M.–12:00 P.M. Sat

Lafayette Cemetery #1 received its first body in 1833 after having been a sugar plantation. As part of a divorce settlement, Madame Jacques François Livaudais had been awarded most of the land that today constitutes the Garden District and the Lafayette Cemetery. When she moved to Paris, Madame Livaudais sold the land for a sweet $490,000.

Lafayette is the oldest city-owned (i.e., non–Catholic Archdiocese-owned) cemetery in New Orleans. It is sometimes called the "American" cemetery because it's not predominantly French or Spanish like other cemeteries. It holds the remains of citizens from 25 different countries. Also unlike most cemeteries in New Orleans, Lafayette was never segregated by race, ethnicity, or religious denomination.

There are about 1,100 family tombs and more than 7,000 people buried in Lafayette Cemetery #1, but fewer renowned residents than in St. Louis #1. The most famous in Lafayette are fictional ones. The tomb for the Mayfair witches, created by Anne Rice in *The Witching Hour*, was set here. Anne Rice also staged her own jazz funeral and mock burial here, when she rode in a glass-enclosed coffin down the aisle of Lafayette Cemetery to launch her book *Memnoch the Devil*. Vampire Lestat's tomb, made from Styrofoam, was nestled in Lafayette for the filming of *Interview with the Vampire*. Many other movies have been filmed in the cemetery, including *The Skeleton Key*, *Double Jeopardy* (where Ashley Judd was shoved inside a vault), and *Dracula 2000* (filmed, appropriately, in 2000). LeAnn Rimes and the New Kids on the Block have filmed music videos here.

This cemetery is the only one in New Orleans dedicated to an individual. Theodore Von LaHache's dedication plaque hangs below the front gate. He was Roman Catholic organist, composer, music teacher, founder of the New Orleans Philharmonic Society, and owner of a music store. When alive, he was the best-known musician in New Orleans. I learned from one tour guide that LaHache is now solely remembered for his composition of "The Daring Young Man on the Flying Trapeze." I learned from Google that my tour guide was just making stuff up. Gaston Lyle wrote that song.

Many of those buried in Lafayette #1 died in epidemics that swept through the city in the 1800s. Through three outbreaks, the total dead from yellow fever in New Orleans exceeded 41,000. Some of the less graphic symptoms (black vomit, bleeding from the eyes) included a slowing of the metabolism to a barely detectable pulse. Many yellow fever victims were assumed dead and buried alive. This included the mother of Jefferson Davis, president of the Confederacy, stored overnight in Lafayette.

Davis's momma got out alive from her tomb, just a little worse for wear, because of two practices commonly used at the time. Back in these more primitive times, dead bodies were merely laid to rest inside the family vaults without preparation. Morticians did not yet in use the current and more civilized modern procedures, whereby they slash the carotid artery and jugular vein and suck out all the blood and replace it with 3 gallons of an embalming cocktail of formaldehyde, methanol, and ethanol. Instead, a small bell would be tied to the finger so that if the "dead" suddenly woke up inside their burial vault, they could ring the bell, alerting outsiders to the fact, "Hey! I'm not quite dead yet." Thus the phrases *dead ringer* and *saved by the bell*. The first few nights, someone, usually a slave, would be posted outside the vault to listen for the bell. Thus the phrase *graveyard shift*.

If you take the Canal Street streetcar line, aptly named "Cemeteries," to the end, there is a cluster of Cypress Grove Cemetery, Odd Fellows, Greenwood, St. Patrick's, and the Metairie Cemetery. Hidden behind a gas station and flower shop is the Katrina Memorial, built in 2007 on top of what used to be the Charity Hospital Cemetery (5050 Canal Street).

Once again, the numbers placed in front of Metairie's residents refer to the map of the grounds.

Lake Lawn Metairie Cemetery
LOCATION: 5100 Pontchartrain Blvd. (at Rte. 10 and City Park Ave.)
HOURS: 7:30 A.M.–5:30 P.M. 7 days a week

The Metairie Cemetery is New Orleans' most photo-friendly cemetery, with the largest collection of marble tombs, some with stained-glass windows, noted funeral statuary like the *Weeping Angel*, and unlike the congested and arbitrary design of St. Louis #1, Metairie is a drive-thru cemetery with wide and open vistas. It also has a storied history.

In the mid-1800s it was the site of a country club and racetrack, a popular

The Weeping Angel

Alexey Sergeev

place with the wealthy elite. The club refused to allow Charles T. Howard to become a member because he was nouveau riche and, worse, a Yankee. In response to his rebuke, Charles T. vowed that he would one day buy the privileged club and then besmirch its memory by turning it into a cemetery.

As money grew tight after the Civil War, many of those supporting the club fell on hard times, and soon enough the racetrack was put up for sale. Poetically, Charles T. Howard bought it and followed up on his promise to turn it into a graveyard.

The cemetery has become the final resting spot for many who would have been more than welcomed into the country club and racetrack. There are 11 Louisiana governors, 9 New Orleans mayors, dozens of Confederate officers, and an area called Millionaire's Row, so named because it costs so much to be buried in this prime real estate section. Stating, "Eventually everyone will end up somewhere. I guess it's the last house I'll buy," attorney Ray Brandt paid over a million dollars for an eight-crypt mausoleum for his family. Here are some of the other must-see landmarks:

 By far the tallest monument on the property is the obelisk marked "Moriarty." It's the first thing you'll see up front at the corner nearest Route 10. It is tallest structure by design. Daniel Moriarty emigrated from Ireland and married Mary Farrell. Although he and his wife accumulated great wealth, they were never accepted into upper-class society because they didn't have generational New Orleans bloodlines. When Mary died in 1887, Daniel used some of his wealth to erect a monument from which she could look down upon all the society snobs buried near her tomb. The four statues at the base of the pillar are said to be Faith, Hope, Charity, and Mrs. Moriarty.

 Louisiana Division–Army of Tennessee is a 30-foot-high tumulus (burial mound), topped by a bronze statue of General Albert Sidney Story in a pose described to the sculptor as how Story had looked in the moments before he died charging the Yankees in the first hours of the Battle of Shiloh. Story himself was buried here only briefly before his body was moved to the Texas State Cemetery.

General Pierre Gustave Toutant-Beauregard is still buried here. "The Little Creole" or "Little Napoleon" as he was called at different times, was a native New Orleanian who singlehandedly started the

Civil War when he ordered the first shots fired on Fort Sumter. Speaking only French in New Orleans, he didn't learn a word of English until he was a teenager and sent to New York for education. He graduated second in his class at West Point. Four years of pain, Sherman's march to the sea, and 618,222 lost lives could have been averted had the little general never learned English and instead yelled "*Feu à volonté*!" to his befuddled Rebel troops. After the war, he was active in campaigning for voting rights and education for freed slaves.

 The most famous and most photographed statue in the cemeteries of New Orleans is the *Weeping Angel*, bowed inside the family vault constructed by Charles Hyams. Hyams was a stockbroker, art collector, and philanthropist who helped create the city's art museum in 1911 by donating many of his paintings. The statue of the angel is a replica of a stylized tomb first used in Rome. There are now some 40 weeping angel statues all over the world, including in Luxembourg, Costa Rica, and Quebec, and nine in Texas alone.

Josie Arlington was an infamous madam from Storyville. Her brothel, which she named the Chateau Lobrano d'Arlington to class it up, was especially popular because she fired more common whores and brought in a wealth of educated foreign girls. They commanded a then outrageous price of five dollars an hour. The going rate back then was 22 cents per hour. The brothel also offered 10 to 12 girls in a live "sex circus" in which patrons could participate or pay merely to watch. Josie provided specially trained ladies for fetishists and sadomasochists. All for a price, of course.

Learning she intended to be buried in Metairie Cemetery, a cartel of society women were mortified that such a person would be buried near their husbands or fathers and sought to block her. Josie responded, "I wonder how many of these ladies know their husbands visit me weekly."

With all her money, she did get in. Near the front of the cemetery, Josie was interned in a beautiful red granite tomb with carved burning urns and a bronze statue of a woman reaching for the door. There have been some strange happenings at the tomb over the years. Two grave-diggers swore they saw the statue walk away one night. Others have claimed they've seen granite flames burst into real fire.

Under steady and heavy protests, the cemetery did finally agree to remove her remains. The mausoleum today is etched in the names of just one family, ironically Morales, the Spanish word for virtue and moral correctness.

⚜ Mel Ott was the Hall of Fame baseball player who played for and managed his entire career for the then New York Giants, now San Francisco. "Master Melvin" was the six-time home run leader and the first National League player to reach five hundred home runs. Trying to pitch around his bat, Mel Ott also led the majors in being intentionally walked six years running.

⚜ Al Hirt, the son of a New Orleans police officer, was given his first trumpet when he was six years old. He went on to become a world-famous musician. While primarily a jazz trumpet player, Al was classically trained, receiving his doctorate in performing arts from the Cincinnati Conservatory of Music, and performing all kinds of music, even with symphony orchestras. He was a Grammy winner and inductee to the International Jazz Hall of Fame. Hirt's rotund face (he was nicknamed "Jumbo") became synonymous with New Orleans music. He appeared in numerous movies and TV shows, most often asked to play "When the Saints Go Marching In."

⚜ Stan Rice, Anne's poet-artist husband, is buried here. Someday Anne will be, too. While hopefully many years in the future, I don't doubt for a moment Goth kids and vampire lovers will make this the second-most-visited grave in New Orleans (after Marie Laveau's) once she takes up residence. Interestingly, the site is a stone's throw from Al Copeland's. Al, the Popeye's Chicken King, and Anne were much ballyhooed enemies, tossing full-page invective at each other in the local papers.

⚜ Andrew Higgins was an industrialist and shipbuilder credited by Dwight Eisenhower as the "man who won the war for us." During World War II, he designed and manufactured the ramp-bow Eureka boat, the LCVP (landing craft, vehicle, personnel), or simply, the Higgins Boat, used to deliver troops to the beaches of Normandy on D-Day. He is also a primary reason the World War II Museum is located in New Orleans.

In 2014, the museum recorded its four-millionth visitor to boost its local economy by four million admission fees.

✠ Ruth Fertel is as much a part of the city's restaurant culture as Emeril Lagasse, John Besh, and others perhaps better known to outsiders. In 1965, ignoring the advice of her friends, lawyer, and banker, Ruth became the seventh owner of Chris Steak House, founded in 1927. She knew nothing about the restaurant business and immediately faced a bit of a crisis when she realized she'd spent all her money buying the restaurant and hadn't budgeted any additional money she'd need to buy food. She would eventually grow the business to being one of the largest steak house chains in America.

   Miss Ruth had to teach herself how to butcher steak, and would saw 30-pound short loins by hand until she could afford an electric band saw. She staffed her restaurant with single mothers, like herself. For many years, Chris Steak House was the only upscale restaurant in New Orleans with an all-female wait staff. In addition to hiring single mothers, Ruth created the first, and then only, fine-dining establishment where blacks felt comfortable. A white oilman once approached Ruth Fertel and announced loudly enough to fill the room, "If that boy stays, I'll never eat here again." Ruth replied, "There's the door."

✠ Angelo Brocato's grave site will mean little to most visitors but everything to locals. He came from Sicily to establish the best confection/dessert shop in the city. Opened in 1905, the shop (214 N. Carrollton Avenue) is still run by his heirs. Angelo Brocato's ice-cream parlor serves gelato, biscotti, torrone, frutta Marturana, and its famed cannoli Siciliana, made by hand while you watch. My daughter Ella and I feel compelled to leave a little something by Angelo's grave each time we pass by. She's changed her favorite flavor from raspberry to chocolate; I've stayed committed to strawberry cheesecake gelato. Marnie has commitment issues and splits her choices among the Baci, Sicilian pistachio nut, and pear ice granita.

✠ Louis Prima was a singer, actor, songwriter, trumpeter, and owner of a nightclub on Bourbon Street. At his height of popularity, he had a number of top hits, like "The Lady in Red," "I Ain't Got Nobody," and

"Just a Gigolo." His most lasting is probably "I Wanna Be Like You" from Prima's voice-over role as King Louie the orangutan in Disney's animated *The Jungle Book*.

Prima was a bit of a gigolo, blowing through huge sums of money on expensive suits and at the racetrack. He married a succession of three women, each in her teens when he married her.

His gray marble crypt is topped by a figure of Gabriel, the trumpeter-angel. The inscription on the crypt's door quotes the lyrics from his hit song: "When the end comes, I know, they'll all say 'just a gigolo' as life goes on without me." Visitors leave pennies at the foot of his tomb as a reference to another Prima hit song, "Pennies from Heaven."

⚜ Jefferson Davis, the president of the Confederacy, died in the home of friend Jacob U. Payne at First and Camp Streets. His body was buried in the Metairie Cemetery for three and a half years, before Richmond, Virginia, demanded he be brought back to the once Confederate capital. I'm guessing at that point Mister Jeff's remains could have been transported to Virginia in a picnic basket.

⚜ Owen Brennan is the great patriarch of New Orleans restaurants. Currently 10 restaurants are run by heirs to the empire: Commander's Palace, Ralph's on the Park, Dickie Brennan's Steak House, Palace Cafe, Tableau, and others, and by the time this book hits the shelves, the original Brennan's will be reopened having been passed from Pip Brennan to Ralph Brennan by way of a bevy of lawyers and bad blood. Owen himself was a bigger-than-life gregarious showman, goaded into creating New Orleans signature restaurant by "Count" Arnaud Cazenave (Arnaud's) who made the snarky comment that an Irishman wouldn't be able to run anything better than a hamburger joint.

⚜ Jim Garrison was an overzealous district attorney who screwed up the evidence and failed to prove conspiracy in the murder of JFK. He then forever screwed up Bourbon Street when he delivered on a campaign promise to clean it up. He swept out the burlesque houses, removing the merely risqué and leaving a void filled by the much raunchier strip joints you'll find today. There was, back then, not much to clean up. Performer Blaze Starr had a tabloid affair with the governor. So what?

Their affair led to another of my favorite quotes from New Orleans history. Earl Long: "Would you still love me as much if I wasn't the fine governor of the great state of Louisiana?" Blaze Starr: "Would you still love me if I had little tits and worked in a fish house?"

Greenwood Cemetery
LOCATION: 5200 Canal Blvd. (that's Blvd., not St.)
HOURS: 8:00 A.M.–4:00 P.M. 7 days a week

The cemetery is owned by the Firemen's Charitable and Benevolent Association, and bills itself as "still the best value in town." Personally, in my unjustifiable opinion, other than the large bronze elk that greets you, it's one of the more visually boring spaces. The landscape is laid out in perfect rows on a grid pattern, all mausoleums looking pretty much alike. But it does hold two of New Orleans' more eccentric characters.

Ruth Grace Moulon, better known as Ruthie the Duck Girl, was a French Quarter icon. A tiny woman with a near constant grin (except when she was hurling profanities), she zoomed from bar to bar on roller skates, mooching drinks and cigarettes, wearing a ratty fur coat and long skirt or wedding gown and veil (she considered herself engaged to a sailor who passed through the Quarter in 1963). She was always trailed by a duck or two. Ruthie had legendary status in a city that treasures people far outside the mainstream, sort of an inadvertent tourist attraction.

She made pocket change from people wanting to take her picture with her ducks and by selling postcards of herself, 25 cents per card or three for a dollar. In her offbeat mind, that represented a bargain.

In 1999, Rick Delaup made her the subject of a documentary, *Ruthie the Duck Girl*. You can still buy a copy at the Louisiana Music Factory or www.eccentricneworleans.com. Though basically jobless and homeless much of her life, she acquired a coterie of people who found places for her to live, paid her bills, and made sure she got inside at night. Photographer David Richmond perfectly summed up Ruthie the Duck Girl: "She's not out of touch with reality; she's just not interested."

The more famous Greenwood resident is John Kennedy Toole. He resides on Latanier Row between Magnolia and Hawthorne. The most prominent name on the grave is Ducoing, his mother's maiden name. John wrote *A Confederacy of Dunces*, considered *the* quintessential New Orleans novel. The work details the misadventures of protagonist Ignatius J. Reilly, a lazy, obese, misanthropic, self-styled scholar who lives at home with his mother. All of these descriptions applied quite well to Toole himself.

The novel was published 11 years after his suicide. Suffering from depression and increasing dementia, exacerbated by his novel being repeatedly rejected for publication, Toole took a final bucket list road trip, going to the Hearst mansion in California; then Milledgeville, Georgia, home of writer Flannery O'Connor; and finally Biloxi, Mississippi, where he killed himself at age 31. His mother continued to try to sell her son's masterpiece and eventually captured the enthusiastic attention of Walker Percy. LSU published the novel in 1981. It won that year's Pulitzer Prize for best novel.

True story: Reading about *A Confederacy of Dunces* the week prior to its publication, I thought it sounded fascinating and collectible. I was working in a bookstore in New York and when the novel arrived, I put three of the initial 10 copies aside for myself. The other seven sold out the first day, causing me to order 25 more. Then, I made the mistake of letting one, then two of my set-aside copies go to customers. I said there was no way I'd let the last copy go . . . but the next customer looked like a young Cybill Shepherd. I justified letting her have it with, "There are twenty-five more coming in tomorrow." And I was secretly hoping she'd be so grateful for her book, we'd be living together in a week or two. When the reorder arrived, the novel was already in its fourth printing. Last I looked, first editions were going for $2,500 per copy. I never saw the young Cybill look-alike again.

A Confederacy of Dunces is stuffed to the gills with some of the greatest quotes about New Orleans and about life assembled in one novel. One of my favorites could serve as a description of the novel and an epitaph on Toole's tomb: "I am at the moment writing a lengthy indictment against our century. When my brain begins to reel from my literary labors, I make an occasional cheese dip."

Holt Cemetery

LOCATION: 635 City Park Ave.

HOURS: 8:00 A.M.–2:30 P.M. Mon–Fri; 8:00 A.M.–12:00 P.M. Sun

Within walking distance of the Canal Street Cluster, Holt Cemetery is located right behind Delgado Community College. Holt is New Orleans' most eccentric, anything-goes cemetery. Originally it was a potter's field, or indigent

One of the many unique graves at Holt Cemetery   ALEXEY SERGEEV

cemetery for those who couldn't afford otherwise. The graves are mostly underground with some coping graves—slightly aboveground memorials with boxed frames made from stone, brick, or plaster (in one case, plastic plumbing tubes), and filled with earth up to around 3 feet aboveground—covering the remains.

I have provided no map because we just don't know where many of the residents are buried, and it's totally worth your while to wander around aimlessly. You never know what you'll bump into.

There are two tributes to Buddy Bolden but no known site of his actual grave. One tribute calls him "the blowingest man since Gabriel," a quote from Jelly Roll Morton. Buddy, a.k.a. King Bolden, a victim of acute alcohol psychoses and dementia praecox, spent the last 24 years of his life in the Louisiana State Insane Asylum. But before all that, he's been credited as "the Father of Jazz." Playing by ear, he developed a looser, more improvised version of ragtime and added blues and funk. One of his early hits, "Funky Butt," truly changed the musical landscape. His style was louder and more wide open than anything that came before. Bolden's band was the first to have brass instruments play the blues. He is also credited with the discovery or invention of the so-called Big Four, a key rhythmic innovation on the marching band beat. It created much more room for individual improvisation. The Big Four was the first syncopated bass drum pattern to deviate from the standard on-the-beat march. The second half of the Big Four is the pattern commonly known as habanera rhythm, or basically the New Orleans Sound. Thus, Buddy Bolden, buried who-knows-where in Holt Cemetery, can be considered perhaps the most important musician in New Orleans history, and quite possibly all of America.

While not finding Buddy's grave, you will find a bizarre landscape of stuffed animals: Home Depot–quality statues of Mary, St. Francis, and singing cherubs; plastic flowers; and carpet remnants strewn throughout the cemetery. Miss Thelma Lowe has a coveted Zulu coconut on her grave, and a sea of wonderful hand-carved and/or handwritten headstones, some in magic marker, others in broken-plate mosaic. Emily Lorraine's headstone tells that she died in 2004 and was "bone" on June 20, 1947.

There are a few out-of-the-way, accessible-only-by-car-or-cab cemeteries (unless you *really* like to walk . . . through dicey neighborhoods) where you might want to pay tribute to their renowned residents, or in the case of St. Roch's, heal what ails you.

St. Roch Cemetery

LOCATION: 1725 St. Roch Ave.

HOURS: 8:30 A.M.–4:00 P.M. Mon–Fri; closed Sat and Sun

In 1867 Father Peter Leonard Thevis arrived from Germany to minister to the neighborhood's largely German parish. This was the time of a yellow

Leave-behinds at St. Roch Grotto　　　　　　　ALEXEY SERGEEV

fever outbreak in the city. There were over three thousand deaths the year before. Father Pete gathered his congregation and announced that they would pray to St. Roch, the patron saint of dogs, plague, and pestilence, to intercede on their behalf. When not one parishioner contracted the disease, he began raising money to build a shrine to St. Roch, completed in August 1876.

The grotto to the right of the altar, called the Healing Room, has become one of the coolest, if lesser-known, spots in New Orleans. The small room is filled with tokens of thanks: plaques, abandoned leg braces, crutches, and plaster or cement statues of a previously afflicted body parts—hands, hearts, brains—healed through prayer at St. Roch's.

Outside of the shrine, along the walls are the 14 Stations of the Cross that mark Jesus's crucifixion. The tableaux are life-size, brilliantly white statues against a teal background. Bring your camera and, if you're suffering with a hangover, may I suggest a plaster cast of a brain?

Providence Memorial Park
LOCATION: 8200 Airline Dr., Metairie
HOURS: 9:00 A.M.–2:00 P.M. Mon–Fri, 9:00 A.M.–12 P.M. Sat

Mahalia Jackson was born into poverty, one of six kids in a tiny three-room shotgun apartment in New Orleans. She dropped out of school in the eighth grade to help make money for the family. As a teenager she moved to Chicago to live with her aunt, and there she began singing in the Greater Salem Baptist Church. That, as they say, changed everything. Mahalia Jackson would go on to be the undisputed Queen of Gospel. She continued to wash clothing for a dollar a day and worked at a beauty parlor, which she would eventually own because singing didn't pay the bills. Miss Mahalia earned $25 for her first recording in 1934. In 1946 she recorded her signature song "Move On Up a Littler Higher," which sold 100,000 copies out the gate and eventually passed one million in sales. Her other multimillion-sellers include "In the Upper Room," "Didn't It Rain," "Even Me," and "Silent Night." She recorded about 30 albums during her career and also appeared in the movies *Imitation of Life*, *St. Louis Blues*, *The Best Man* and *I Remember Chicago*. In 1950 she became the first gospel singer to perform at New York's Carnegie Hall, then in 1958 the first to sing at the Newport Jazz Festival. In 1961 she sang at President John F. Kennedy's inauguration. Her singing career took her all over Europe, Asia, and Africa. Back in New Orleans, Miss Mahalia is perhaps best known as the creator of Jazz Fest, which happened when she was in town for a festival in Congo Square and George Wein shoved a microphone in her face and told her, "Sing!" Now in its 45th year, Jazz Fest turns out well over half a million fans each year.

A steady stream of spiritual pilgrims visit Mahalia Jackson's tomb, including busloads of schoolchildren and tourists from as far away as Japan.

Another resident of note is the incomparable James Booker, called "the Bronze Liberace" and considered one of New Orleans' greatest piano players.

Garden of Memories
LOCATION: 4900 Airline Hwy., Metairie
HOURS: 7:30 A.M.–5:30 P.M. 7 days a week

Some charred bits of Cecil Ingram Connor III are in an underground grave marked by a flat stone that features a bas-relief carving of the musician and a verse from "In My Hour of Darkness." Cecil is better known by his professional name, Gram Parsons. Parsons was a pivotal member in influential groups the Byrds, the Flying Burrito Brothers, and the International Submarine Band. The Submarine Band's album *Safe at Home* is considered the first ever country-rock album. *Rolling Stone* magazine lists Parsons as #87 on the top 100 greatest artists of all time.

He died at age 26 from an overdose of alcohol and morphine. His stepfather overruled his wish to be cremated at Joshua Tree National Park. Instead his body was to be flown to New Orleans for burial. However, friends Phil Kaufman and Michael Martin intercepted the body at the LAX airport, drove to Joshua Tree, poured gasoline inside the coffin, and set it on fire. The resulting fireball alerted police and led to a high-speed chase. The two were arrested but eventually fined only $700 with no jail time. The remaining remains were finally interred in the Garden of Memories.

The cemetery's senior communications specialist said the Garden of Memories doesn't keep track of the volume of sightseers to Parsons's grave and can't comment on the subject without the consent of family members. The cans of High Life beer left at the site attest to the fact that he is receiving at least some visitors.

Mount Olivet Cemetery

LOCATION: 4000 Norman Mayer Ave.

HOURS: 8:00 A.M.–4:30 P.M. Mon–Fri, 8:00 A.M.–1:00 P.M. Sat

Located in the Gentilly neighborhood, Mount Olivet will probably be the most distant for most visitors and be surrounded by the least points of interest, though there is a McKenzie's Chicken in a Box nearby.

Still, many make the pilgrimage to honor Henry Roeland "Roy" Byrd, better known to the world as Professor Longhair, or "Fess" for short. Cemetery employees say he gets three to five visitors every day.

He has been hailed as "the Picasso of keyboard funk" and "the Bach of rock." Fess is in the Rock and Roll Hall of Fame. His musical notoriety is based on his way offbeat songs and instantly identifiable piano style, which he once described as a blend of "rumba, mambo, and calypso." His sound served to profoundly influence all New Orleans pianists that came after him, including Mac Rebennack (a.k.a. Dr. John), Fats Domino, Huey "Piano" Smith, James Booker, and Allen Toussaint.

As a child, he would dance on Bourbon Street for nickels and dimes: He found a broken piano in an alleyway and began banging around. Byrd's self-taught, idiosyncratic style became the signature freewheeling rhythms of the Crescent City. Fess soaked up the many influences from all the sources within earshot: barrelhouse boogie-woogie, Caribbean rhythms like the rumba (many of his relatives were West Indian), and the second line parade rhythms, all stirred together in his one-of-a-kind and revolutionary pocky way.

Fess put together a band where all the members had long hair and were thereby referred to as "Professor Longhair and the Four Hairs." He recorded and toured for a decade, then poor health required he remain in New Orleans for the next 15 years, performing and recording intermittently. His irregular gigs were never enough to support him. For a time, he was a part-owner at Jimmy Hicks's Barbecue Pit, where he cooked and fronted a gambling operation. He later worked at One Stop recording studios, but sweeping floors rather than making music.

By 1970, Longhair's recordings had circulated around the world to his becoming a piano legend in Europe and the subject of adoring articles in blues magazines. Locally, he came to the attention of Allison Miner Kaslow, who worked at the Tulane Jazz Archive, and Quint Davis, who was just beginning to produce the New Orleans Jazz & Heritage Festival. Both spent months searching everywhere for the man, but it was Davis who tracked Longhair down at One Stop. "He wasn't playing at all then," said Davis. "He was in a totally depreciated state physically, along with poverty and rejection. But he always had this great spirit to endure no matter what. He was living in a little house without a pot to piss in and ready to start over with nothing for an unknown public. He really believed he could have a reincarnation. So I followed up and got him to play the Jazz Festival at Congo Square."

His appearance at the 1971 Jazz Fest was the turning point in Longhair's career. "The first time I saw him he came hobbling through Congo Square," said the late Kaslow. "He was wearing a suit that had been pressed so many times that it shined. But when he played it was like nothing I'd ever heard before. Byrd was so hip and full of energy. I couldn't believe here was all this talent seemingly going to waste."

Poor health coupled with, quite frankly, a sound and style that wasn't meant for mass appeal and sold-out stadiums, made him unable to tour. An ambitious group of young New Orleanians, led by Henry "Hank" Drevich, pulled together enough money to buy a club where he'd always have a place to play. The old 501 Club on Tchoupitoulas and Napoleon Streets was renamed Tipitina's in honor of a Professor Longhair song supposedly inspired by a woman with no toes who sold marijuana.

Mount Olivet is also the final resting place of musicians Shirley & Lee, former teen doo-wop stars ("I'm Gone," "Feels So Good"), and rapper Soulja Slim.

That-Which-Must-Not-Be-Named
LOCATION: **Unknown**
HOURS: **???**

I hesitate to write this final cemetery entry, but there's also a for-those-in-the-know cemetery gate (I know its name, but dare not write it down) that serves as a portal to the dead. The exact location of the haunted cemetery gates is never told to outsiders. Cemetery or ghost tour guides will skirt around the issue, or just look at you like they don't know what you're talking about. They say just to talk about the accursed cemetery gates spells doom to those who speak of it openly.

However, if you're an Odd Fellow walking down the widest street in America, you just might find it. To find these gates, they say, is to find the

Get the Grave Decorator

Following the assassination of JFK, while other reporters and media hounds rushed to Dallas or DC to get the story, Jimmy Breslin chose to go to the Arlington National Cemetery to interview Clifton Pollard, the man who dug the grave to receive the president's body. His column in the *New York Herald Tribune* became an instant classic and created the journalistic term *get the gravedigger*. It refers to getting to the heart of a major news story through creative and intuitive side angles rather than obvious ones.

In my attempt to literally get the gravedigger and interview a groundskeeper for a cemetery, I made the mistake of approaching the Archdiocese. I was quickly rebuffed. "I'm sure you're aware of the Catholic faith and the reverence we place in our Catholic Cemeteries. We need to decline your request for being part of the book dealing with voodoo, vampires, graveyards and ghosts." They then helpfully added, "You may be able to get a worker from one of city cemeteries to help you," intimating the godless frivolity of non-Catholic cemeteries.

Trying to get the gravedigger through more clandestine means, I ended up chasing phantoms. A private tour guide, hanging out by a cemetery, led me to his friend who was supposedly a retired cemetery groundskeeper. I could only reach the gravedigger through the tour guide, as the digger had no phone or e-mail. I then discovered the tour guide's phone had been disconnected, too. Long story short, I did eventually track down the alleged gravedigger and met him early one morning at his house in a somewhat "questionable" neighborhood. I was, however, delighted by the inside of his home. There were little altars everywhere. There were shrines to deceased friends and he'd strung up stuffed animals on the walls in peculiar handmade outfits. One toy monkey had on high-heeled boots, and a little bra and panties with glued-on hearts.

Over breakfast—he made me eggs, grits, fried fish, and toast from the oven—he told me tales from his years in the business. He seems to have known everyone from Uncle Lionel to Ernie K-Doe. Former mayor Marc Morial supposedly owed him favors, and Kermit Ruffins got him fired. The alleged gravedigger had been a mule-drawn carriage driver/tour guide who used to take a young Kermit and his band members around the Quarter, playing their music and telling fans where they'd next appear. The carriage company did not approve.

The alleged gravedigger then showed me a photograph on his wall of his taking the Obama family on a carriage ride. The driver was clearly the man in whose kitchen I sat. The family in the backseat was clearly the Obamas. But just as clear was the fact that the Obama picture had been cut out of a magazine and pasted on.

The alleged gravedigger presently makes his money as a tour guide, or rather, as he insisted, an information provider. He doesn't have a tour guide license, so cannot accept set payments for giving tours. He can, however, take tips for dispensing information. He's also been a cab driver and an amateur lawyer. He represented himself on a charge of throwing a brick into City Hall. The alleged gravedigger allegedly got off by proving he was already *inside* City Hall and therefore he threw the brick *out* of City Hall, not *in*. I eventually got to ask at what point had he been a gravedigger. He told me it was . . . well, never.

Thankfully, in New Orleans, in addition to gravediggers we also have grave decorators. As is the case with so much in New Orleans, we're just different. In most American cemeteries, idiosyncratic monuments and decorations any more strange than plastic flowers are discouraged or even prohibited. Where my parents are buried, the only variety from one grave to the next is the etched-in-stone Methodist cross, or Episcopalian cross, or Catholic one. The cemeteries of New Orleans allow residents extravagantly more license to embellish burial places.

Some New Orleans cemeteries do require that grave sites be kept reasonably tidy. A family can even pay to have its site swept clean of leaves, spiderwebs, or Mardi Gras beads. You'll see "Perpetual Care" plaques embedded in the ground in front of these graves. But in other cemeteries, like Holt, anything goes.

In the traditional religions of Africa, from where the original slaves arrived, great reverence is shown for the dead. Ancestral spirits serve as guides and advisers to the living and are believed to withhold their assistance or even cause harm if they are not properly honored with regular offerings.

In African American cemeteries, not just New Orleans, but stretching from Louisiana to the South Carolina Low Country, family and friends leave personal objects that belonged to the dead for their use in the spirit world. When the dead call out, "Leave me somethin', mister!" they want more than handwritten eulogies or Mardi Gras beads. Left-behinds include cups and saucers, candy dishes, pitchers, medicine bottles, figurines, clocks, auto parts, and bed frames. The dishes and medicine bottles must be cracked so that the spirit inside the objects are released to serve the former owner in the next world.

This practice probably leads back to the Congo in Central Africa. Needed utensils like cooking pots, crockery, and glass bottles were placed on graves there to ensure that the spirit would not come stumbling into the homes of the living. In both Africa and the American South, seashells are often left at graves. Shells symbolize the water from whence the spirits came and to which they now return.

A practice called Dumb Supper is clearly related to African rituals. Practitioners place two plates and wineglasses by a grave and call up the dead with offerings of bread, wine, rum, cigars, or a bag of chips if they're hard up. If the spirits show up, they'll provide sought-after answers from the other side.

The X's you'll find all over Marie Laveau's tomb, among others, is also rooted in African tradition. The two crossed lines represent the intersection between the realm of the living and the realm of the spirit. The custom, unique to New Orleans, of drawing X's on grave markers is related to Haitian Vodou practice called *kwasiyen*. Signing with an X is used to establish contact with the *lwa*, or Vodou deities.

Arthur Raymond Smith began decorating cemetery sites in November 1978 after the death of his mother. His work has nothing to do with any ancient rituals, except perhaps in some sort of Jungian collective unconscious kind of way. With the death of his mother, Arthur had the inspiration to decorate his mother's grave in the Carrollton Cemetery and also his grandmother's in St. Louis #1. It was his way to honor the two women who had the greatest influence in his life and make a final connection with their spirit.

Arthur said of his grandmother, "She spent her life caring for our family at home while my mother worked to support us. When I was a child I suffered terribly from asthma, and she doctored me with home remedies. I keep this memorial to her out of love and gratitude." He was born, grew up, and has always lived in rough neighborhoods, where he was protected by the two strong women. The bricks he stacks at grave sites is a nod to the practice of his mother's placing bricks all over the front steps to keep drug addicts from perching near the house. His grandmother taught him to avoid eye contact with riffraff strolling the streets and Arthur passed along to me to not even say no when street people ask for change. "Once they engage you, they got you." In his neighborhoods, he lives by his grandmother's code: "Hello and goodbye are for dogs and for cats, or for roaches and rats." Don't be talking to strangers.

Arthur is a hoarder of epic proportions. Over decades, he used to gather and save fencing, bits of wire, ribbon, beads, discarded stuffed animals, fake flowers, colorful plastic shopping bags, seashells, old bricks, carpet remnants, shopping carts (while I sat with Arthur, a woman I'm guessing he knew came up and asked if she could have one of his shopping carts, to which he gracefully agreed), and religious objects. For my interview with Arthur, I'd gathered a coffee tin of stuff I'd found around my house, to present for future decorations: a small chalk statue of a woman praying, a button with the pyramid and all-seeing eye, a small wooden mask of a tiger, a child's letter block, and a multicolored sequence patch decorated to be an Indian elephant. I'd considered, but couldn't part with, a wooden foot model for a child's shoe, a plastic acupuncture ear, a Shriner bobble-headed doll, a glass eyeball, a statue of St. Lucy holding her tray of eyeballs, or any from my collection of hundreds of statues of men in business suits. I'm a bit of a hoarder, too.

Arthur Raymond Smith

Arthur's hoarding got so intense that he was evicted from his former home in the Marigny. The house, plus most of his collection, was destroyed because it had become infested with rats—so much so that Arthur stopped sleeping there and spent nights at a homeless shelter or on the street. He only managed to save a handful of photographs and obituary notices, all of which he has plastic wrapped and carries with him like an amulet bag.

Sitting on his front stoop in Central City, he showed me everything left of his possessions. Hopefully Arthur, who will turn 82 before *Fear Dat* is published, will still be around so I can give him a copy of the book with this profile to add to his collection.

Over the years, he has worked as a handyman, butler, dishwasher, insurance agent, photographer, florist, door-to-door sales agent for the Fuller Cosmetics Company, and very briefly, in the 1960s, he opened his own church, based on his strictly personal interpretation of Christianity. He is now unemployed. You can spot Arthur shuffling around New Orleans with a grocery cart in which he salvages recyclable bottles and cans for quick cash and collects discards that interest him for his grave-site decorations.

He's become something of a celebrity among New Orleans collectors of "outsider" and "visionary" art. New Orleans historian Rob Florence and artist Leslie Staub arranged for an Arthur Smith exhibit at LeMieux Gallery in the Warehouse District that specializes in southern, particularly New Orleans–related, folk art. Arthur came to the opening dressed in a new outfit purchased for the occasion. He charmed the patrons, sold everything on display, and left with several hundred dollars cash. The Florences offered to send him home in a taxi, but he preferred to walk the rather long distance and stop at a bar for a celebratory drink. "That night," Smith said, "I felt like I'd won the Academy Award."

You can see his art today at St. Louis #1, where he decorated his first tomb at the family vault that holds his grandmother, Amanda Dorsey. The tomb was purchased in 1927 for only $45 when his grandfather died. Amanda was buried there after her death in 1945.

When you enter the cemetery gate, look to your left. Along the oven wall, fourth grave in, you'll have no doubt which one is Amanda's. Amid a sea of sun-bleached white, hers is all blue and pink painted, with ever-changing adornments. When I was last there, he'd left old bricks to hold down clear sheets covering brightly colored plastic letters, probably from a child's magnetic board for learning to spell. Apparently he needs to find one more plastic A, as the sign read "Aminda Dorsey Boswell Birthday November-14-1892 Death November-3-1945 At Rest At Peace."

Past installations have included plastic jugs of fresh flowers, a miniature garden of potted plants, wire fencing, and a brick encased in a plastic wrapper with the printed slogan, "Make It a Memory." Most often you'll find photocopied and enlarged portraits of Amanda in a wide-brimmed hat, which Arthur has hand colored.

His artwork has greater expression at the Carrollton Cemetery, where his mother, Ethel Boswell Davis, is buried, and much more so in the Holt Cemetery. Holt Cemetery, on City Park Avenue behind the parking lot of Delgado College, was originally a burial ground for the indigent. Here, people other than Arthur have crafted handmade and hand-lettered markers. Some graves are covered with Astroturf and decorated with cans of beer, rubber duckies, bingo cards. Even here, Arthur Smith's work stands out. He'd used baby bed railing and wire garden fencing to surround the grave, topped it with red shag carpet, a tangle of lawn chairs, bicycle wheels, and various other artifacts with a large plastic owl as the centerpiece.

Nobody seems to know who is buried in all the graves he tends. Arthur considers his work here to be memorial chapels for all the dead of Holt Cemetery.

Lately, he's been placing colored portraits of himself as a young man alongside those of his mother and grandmother. They're labeled "Arthur Raymond Smith Gravesite." Now that he is in his 80s, he said he feels ever closer to the spirit world, and is ready to go when called. Arthur told me he wants to be buried on top of his mother. In our aboveground cemeteries, you are not buried next to your loved ones, but on top of them.

Arthur told me he looks forward to "seeing all the departed people, my own self."

way to communicate openly with the dead. Speak the name of the deceased you wish to speak to aloud five times (or two more than Beetlejuice) through the bars, and they will come and speak to you from the other side. One warning though: If the rusted shut gate creaks open, do not enter. You will be trapped in the world between the living and the dead forevermore. If you arrive and the gates are already open, immediately turn and walk away (quickly) crossing yourself three times. Maybe toss in a few Hail Marys, and for heaven's sake, don't look back.

Le Vampire *by Philip Burne-Jones, 1897*

CHAPTER 3

Vampires

When other little girls wanted to be ballet dancers, I kind of wanted to be a vampire. —**Angelina Jolie, actor and French Quarter resident**

I have never met a vampire personally, but I don't know what might happen tomorrow.
—**Bela Lugosi, actor and permanent resident**
Holy Cross Cemetery, Culver City, CA, Plot: Grotto, L12

E nough about cemeteries and dead people. Let's spend some time with the *un*dead. Vampire tales date back at least to the ancient Egyptians. But New Orleans is the modern-day vampire capital. If you like to dress up like a vampire or if you think you really *are* a vampire, this is the place where you'll feel most at home. New Orleans definitely embraces this most alternative of alternative lifestyles.

Bram Stoker's *Dracula* is the most famous and, in my opinion, the best vampire of all time. Sorry, Edward Cullen, being a moony 104-year-old high school junior makes you considerably less frightening. It's not your fault. Ninety years of high school gym class would drive anyone to say schmaltzy things like, "If I could dream at all, it would be about you."

I assume every reader of this book already knows Bram Stoker based his Dracula on Romanian prince Vlad Tepes, a.k.a. Vlad the Impaler. Vlad was murdered in 1476 and his tomb is, predictably, reported as empty. But vampire mythology seems to go all the way back to ancient Sumerian and Babylonian myths about an *ekimmu*, or one who is not buried properly and returns as a vengeful spirit to suck the life out of the living. In the text of the Egyptian Book of the Dead, *Pert em Hru*, if not all five parts of the soul receive specified offerings, the unattended piece will wander out of the tomb as a *kha* to find nourishment, often by drinking the blood of the living. The ancient Chinese had *jianshi*, or blood-drinking wrathful deities. India had the fanged goddess Kali.

New Orleans vampire lore began in the late 1800s, when young French girls arrived at the Old Ursuline Convent, getting off the boat with all their belongings in a single coffin-shaped suitcase. They'd been sent over to provide proper wives for the male French settlers. Previously, young Frenchmen, deprived of young women, risked life and scalp when they went out into the wilds to cruise for Choctaw chicks. Getting a hatchet buried into your skull is among the worst forms of STD. Collectively, the girls from France were called *filles à la cassette* (girls with a casket), shortened to "casket girls."

The little coffin-suitcases were stored in the convent's attic on the third floor. When some of the suitcases were found to be empty, rather than thinking the girls' possessions had been stolen, hyperimaginative residents began circulating stories that the "casket girls" had smuggled vampires into New Orleans.

Adding to the Ursuline story, the third-floor shutters where the caskets were stored are, to this day, bolted and permanently shut. Why would this be? Certainly not merely to keep the shutters from being ripped off during hurricane-force winds and slicing through the streets of the French Quarter like ballistic missiles. That's too obvious. More active imaginations believe the real reason shutters are bolted must be to keep the vampires inside.

In 1978, two amateur reporters requested to see the coffins on the third floor. Just as the Archdiocese denied me access to cemetery groundskeepers, it rebuffed these two men. Undaunted, the two climbed over the Ursuline Convent wall, and in the courtyard, set up a secret recon station with recording devices. The next day, their equipment was found strewn across the lawn. The two men were found dead on the porch steps. These murders have never been solved.

In addition to introducing vampires to New Orleans, Ursuline was also the first school in America to teach girls and later the first to teach Native Americans and African Americans. Nuns from France were sent to America to serve as instructors for girls, either at the request of Thomas Jefferson or by the decree of King Louis XV, depending on which Google entry you choose to believe. The bodies of the original nuns are buried under the floorboards of Ursuline's music room.

It wasn't just New Orleanians grown hypersensitive about vampires. Much of Europe was, at the time, obsessed with vampires almost to the point of mass hysteria. The vampire myth seems to have really taken hold in Slavic countries back in the 1700s.

The first incident of a real person's being described as a vampire concerned Jure Grando, a peasant in the village of Khring in Croatia. He died in 1656 but was supposedly seen returned from the dead to drink the blood of the locals and sexually harass his widow. Being sexually harassed—by your own husband, after he's dead—that's a bitch. Jure's body was dug up and a stake driven through his no-longer-beating heart. He was seen again by a townsperson, Jure was dug up a second time and his head was cut off. That seemed to do the trick.

During the 18th century, a.k.a. the Age of Enlightenment (?), there was a frenzy of vampire sightings in eastern Europe, with ever-increasing grave diggings to spot-check for vampires and driving stakes into the hearts of decaying mortal remains, just in case.

Widespread panic began with two famous vampire cases, involving the corpses of Petar Blagojevich and Arnold Paole, both from Serbia. Blagojevich was reported to have returned after his death to ask his son for food. When the son refused, he was found dead the following day. Blagojevich supposedly returned repeatedly to attack his former neighbors, who all died from loss of blood. In the second case, after Paole's death, people began to die in the surrounding area. One of Paole's former neighbors was dug up for a look-see. When her body, bloated with gases, looked more nourished than she ever did in life, and there was blood around her mouth (both now recognized attributes of decomposition), she was "proven" to be a vampire. Out came the stakes and off with her head.

From our distant, more enlightened 21st-century perspective (when nearly half of Americans believe in creationism and 25 percent, that the Sun orbits the Earth), we can see that symptoms from then common diseases were misinterpreted as signs of vampirism. The black plague and vomiting blood had given way to tuberculosis, or consumption, as it was called. Victims were slowly consumed, as if they were nightly having their lifeblood sucked out of them. Common tuberculosis symptoms include red, swollen, light-sensitive eyes, pale skin, a weakened heartbeat, and the coughing-up of blood, all of which line up perfectly with common characteristics of vampires.

Other disease and illnesses have vampirelike characteristics. Porphyria is a rare disease characterized by irregularities in production of heme, an iron-rich pigment in blood. The person suffering from porphyria becomes extremely sensitive to light, skin lesions may develop, and the teeth become brown or reddish-brown. The gums recede, giving the canine teeth a fang-like look.

A psychological condition known as Renfield's syndrome, named after the character in Dracula, is also known as clinical vampirism. The patient has the delusion of actually being a vampire and feeling the need for blood. This arises from the erotic attraction to blood and the idea that it conveys certain powers. "The first stage," notes psychologist Richard Noll in his book *Bizarre Diseases of the Mind*, "happens before puberty where the child is excited in a sexual way by some event that involves blood, injury, or the ingestion of blood. At puberty it becomes fused with sexual fantasies, and the typical person with Renfield syndrome begins with autovampirism. That is, they begin to drink their own blood and then move on to other living creatures."

Here in New Orleans, there have been recorded incidents of vampirism, though it's not statistically a leading cause of death. It ranks far behind death from overeating or alcohol poisoning and just ahead of choking on an eye-dropper bottle cap (Tennessee Williams, February 25, 1983).

Our most famous "real" vampire, considerably less famous than the fictional vampires Lestat or Bill Compton, is the Comte de Saint-Germain.

The Comte de Saint-Germain (or Compty as he was known to absolutely no one) was an alchemist who claimed to have the "elixir of life," and to be more than six thousand years old. He was vastly knowledgeable in the sciences and history, and well spoken in many languages, including French, German, Dutch, Spanish, Portuguese, Russian, and English along with familiarity in Chinese, Latin, Arabic, ancient Greek, and Sanskrit. As a great storyteller, Compty became a darling at the court of Louis XV of France.

He was invited to many banquets in the finest homes of Paris, but reportedly, he never ate at a thing. The first record of his suspected immortality was at a party at the manor of Madame de Pompadour. The year was 1760 and a confused guest approached the man she thought was the son of the Compty she knew back in 1710. She discovered it actually was Compty, who hadn't aged a day in 50 years.

Forty years later, the never-aging Comte de Saint-Germain was said to have traveled extensively, continuously dazzling the carriage-setters of Europe (this was before jet-setters). His talents included being a maestro on the violin, a master painter, and deeply knowledgeable of medicine.

Eighteenth-century philosopher Voltaire described Compty as "a man who never dies, and who knows everything."

There were reports he finally died in 1784 in Hamburg, Germany, while he stayed as a guest in the castle at Eckernförde. However, the Comtesse d'Adhémar claims she saw him in Paris nine years later, as part of the Super Bowl–like crowd to witness the beheading of Marie Antoinette.

Years later, in 1902, a man going by the name Jacques Saint Germain moved to New Orleans, into the prestigious building at the corner of Ursulines and Royal. He claimed to have emigrated from the south of France and was a descendent of the Comte de Saint-Germain.

Upon arriving, Jacques threw elaborate parties and invited all the elite dignitaries and politicians of New Orleans. He fed his guests from a catered menu on the finest china and silverware, yet didn't himself eat a bite. Family tradition.

While immensely rich, Jacques never seemed to fit in, neither was he welcomed into the upper-crust society. He was described as charming, highly intelligent, and a master of languages and art, but he was also a party boy, hanging out on Bourbon Street with gangs that would today be the equivalent of football fans whoopin' it up Sugar Bowl weekend.

Out in public, Jacques seemed to have a different young woman on his arm each night. On one cold December evening, he picked up a woman at a local pub and brought her back to his home. Later that night, she flung herself from the second-story window. As bystanders rushed to her aid, she told them how Saint Germain had attacked her. She said he came at her with alarming speed and strength and began biting her viciously on her neck before she broke free and jumped from the window. She died later that evening at Charity Hospital.

When New Orleans police kicked in the door of Saint Germain's home to arrest him, he had already escaped. Inside they discovered large bloodstains in the wooden floor and wine bottles filled with human blood.

There have been numerous and ongoing reports, even in present day, that a mysterious figure, sometimes known as "Jack," will often harass tourists and locals. In 1933, police were summoned to Royal Street where on two consecutive nights young women, assumed to be prostitutes, had their throats torn out. They were completely drained of blood. A witness to the crime claimed they saw a tall figure effortlessly climb a 12-foot wall to make his escape.

ADVENTURES in Apotropaics

It is far harder to kill a phantom than a reality. —Virginia Woolf

Apotropaics are cures to ward off vampires. Apotropaics include the well-known garlic, crucifix, and holy water, but also wild rose, the hawthorn plant, placing mirrors on the outside of doors, and the sprinkling of mustard seeds. Vampires are compulsive counters, so if mustard seeds are spread outside the house, they are compelled to count them all and will waste the entire night away counting ("One! One mustard seed! Two! Two mustard seeds!") and then have to escape the morning sunrise before they ever got around to suck any blood. This part of vampire lore, while it is a part of *Sesame Street*, is absent from most vampire movies and novels. Something about the act of meticulous counting just lacks a certain drama.

Now, getting rid of a vampire has about as many different, very specific, methods and techniques as there have been fad diets claiming how to lose 30 pounds in 30 days. Following are over 20. You may need to use more than one because "killing" something that isn't alive can be tricky.

• The old reliable stake through the heart
Sort of the gold standard for killing a vampire.

• Cutting off the head and placing it at the feet or behind the buttocks
This was, not shockingly, the preferred method in Germany. For best results, use a sword or ax blessed by a priest.

• Exposure to sunlight
An often useless technique if you live in Portland or Seattle.

• Burning
But only as a final step after staking and decapitation. It takes about two days to burn a vampire completely and requires a ton of oil and an endless supply of wood. In one Russian tale "a hundred loads of aspen boughs" were needed to burn one vampire. Plus, you have to kill and burn any animal that ventures near the fire, as the vampire's essence could leap from the fire and use them as a temporary host until finding a new human body.

• Excision of the heart
This technique is not for amateurs. It's rather messy and overall quite unpleasant. The heart is considered to be the part of the vampire that is inhabited by a demonic spirit. Destroy the heart, and you destroy the vampire. (Easier said than done.)

First, the vampire has to be exhumed. Using a sword or knife, the blade having been blessed by a priest, a deep incision is made in the chest. Then, a hand is inserted inside to feel around for the corrupt heart. Once found, the organ is ripped out.

Next, the heart has to be disposed of by burning it completely or boiling it in wine, vinegar, or holy water. The boiled heart or ashes are then returned to the body, with great care taken to spoon every last slag or gob into the body cavity.

This method was actually used on a young woman, Mercy Brown, of Rhode Island in 1892.

• Immersion in water

As lapsed Catholics may remember, water is a symbol of purification and one of the holy sacraments. A vampire fully immersed in water, especially running water, will drown and be destroyed. Do not use a bathtub at home, though. Removing the vampire from the water will revive the creature and then you've got to start the wash cycle all over again.

• Injection with holy water

A hypodermic needle, filled with holy water or holy oil, whichever you prefer, should be inserted into the vampire's heart. This will shoot the consecrated liquid throughout the vampire's body, causing it agonizing pain and eventual death. This is a great method for people who, as kids, used to enjoy burning ants using a magnifying glass and the sun.

• Bottling the vampire

In Bulgarian folklore this is said to be one of the most effective methods of containing and destroying vampires. Basic ingredients are a holy relic or image and a bottle baited with the vampire's favorite food—blood. Then, you go out looking for vampires. Once the vampire is spotted, you will need to chase it, across rooftops, through houses, up trees, or wherever it might flee.

When finally cornered, the vampire is trapped between the crucifix or holy image, and the open bottle of blood. For a vampire, this is a no-brainer. It will choose to take the form of a mist and jump into the bottle, 100 times out of 100. Quickly seal the bottle with a lid (often engraved with a cross). Then throw the bottle into a roaring fire, and pres-to-change-o, no more vampire.

• White wolves

As I'm sure you know, vampires can transform themselves into wolves, bats, CEOs of insurance companies, and college loan officers. But never into white wolves. The white wolf is greatly feared by the vampire. This wolf can sense the undead, and can be extremely useful for tracking vampires. In Albania, the *lugat* (a powerful vampire) can only be destroyed by a white wolf. The wolf does this by biting off the vampire's leg, causing great injury and even greater humil-iation. The *lugat* will retreat to its grave, never to be seen again.

• Shooting with a consecrated bullet

Firearms normally have little or no effect on vampires. However, in one record, a silver bullet that has been blessed by a priest and fired into the vampire's coffin will slay the

Kit for killing a vampire

monster. The writer might have confused methods for killing werewolves. All the same, it is definitely worth a shot, but have a Plan B.

• Stealing the left sock

This one is my absolute favorite. While the vampire sleeps, steal the creature's left sock, ignoring the stench if possible. (There's nothing worse than the smell of eight-hundred-year-old undead feet.) Fill the sock with earth or stones from the vampire's grave and toss the sock as far away as possible. Best if thrown into running water, the deeper the better. The vampire, being intensely OCD as we learned with the mustard seeds, will panic and begin searching frantically for its missing sock. You could even help it along: "Hey Bucky, check the river." Vampires will rush mindlessly into running water to find their sock, but will drown in the process.

This technique is also missing from most vampire movies and novels. After driving a stake through a vampire's heart, cutting off its head, and stuffing it with garlic, I can envision Van Helsing's getting pretty pissed off. "Are you kidding? All I had to do was steal its sock?"

There is also the practice of nailing a suspected vampire to its coffin so it can't rise out, or burying the vampire upside down so if it does dig out, it claws in the wrong direction, getting further and further from the surface. Some buried a suspected vampire corpse with a sickle around its neck so if it sat up it would decapitate itself. Other techniques include putting a thorn under the tongue to prevent it from sucking blood, placing a scooped-out heart on the head, cutting off the feet, shoving a brick in the dead body's mouth, or sewing garlic in the mouth. There's also one the whole family can enjoy: when the body is dismembered, the pieces are burned and the ashes mixed with water, then everyone in the family drinks the mixture so the vampire can't come back to prey on them.

I swear on Bram Stoker's grave all methods just listed are true ways our ancestors actually dealt with vampires. In Bulgaria, over one hundred skeletons have been unearthed with metal objects, such as plow bits, embedded in the torso's chest area, very near where the corrupted heart would have been.

Now, the way you can determine if your deceased Bela or Brumhilda has become a vampire is to have a virgin ride a horse of one color by the grave site. If the horse refuses to walk over the grave, there's definitely a vampire interned beneath the soil.

I am not making this up. (Though clearly someone did.)

About this same time, a terrified young girl entered the police station. She reported two brothers had tied her up and slit her wrist, pouring the blood into a cup and then drinking it. They then bandaged the wound and repeated the feast for the three nights. The police entered the home and found four victims, three alive and a nine-year-old dead. In the next room, they found 17 dead bodies all drained of blood. The blood brothers were captured and executed in the electric chair in 1936. But over the next year, police had more than 20 prowler break-ins reported with descriptions of the two brothers. Their tombs were opened to reveal two empty coffins.

In 1984, nine people were found dead in various locations in French Quarter. All had been murdered by having their throat torn out. All had been drained of blood when the paramedics arrived. These murders remain unresolved more than 30 years later.

A rogue vampire wandered the French Quarter streets in the late 1980s. The police met with the heads of various New Orleans vampire covens, as police in Los Angeles might pressure gang lords to drop the dime on a perp. None of the elders would give up a name but the activity stopped almost immediately.

The most recently recorded vampire attacks on American soil took place in San Francisco in 1998. Joshua Rudiger claimed to be a two-thousand-year-old vampire when he was arrested for slashing the throat of homeless people. But he also claimed to be a Ninja warrior, so maybe he was unmedicated rather than undead.

As the most vampire friendly city in America, New Orleans has many resources for the adventurous undead. The New Orleans Vampire Association (NOVA) describes itself as a "non-profit organization comprised of self-identifying vampires representing an alliance between Houses within the Community in the Greater New Orleans Area. Founded in 2005, NOVA was established to provide support and structure for the vampire and other-kin subcultures and to provide educational and charitable outreach to those in need."

NOVA has been behind the creation of a web series, *Vampires: The Show*, and core members founded Vampsta Vixens in 2011. The Vamp-sta Vixens are a dance/performance group of models, tagged "Beauty with Bite." Founder Lady Dark Adora (somehow that feels like a made-up name), describes the Vixens' evolution, "We began to entertain at the Bad Things monthly parties. It is a fun way to relax, have fun, and meet new people. The Bad Things party became popular and White Wolf of CCP Games used the Bad Things crew, including the Vixens, to perform for an amazing event preparty. Later we performed at the House of Blues in New Orleans for a crowd of over 850 people at the Endless Night Vampire Ball. So far in 2014 we've had shows in Nashville, TN, Austin, TX, and Miami, FL."

Belfazaar Ashantison, or Zaar, (somehow that feels like a made-up name) is a spiritual consultant at Voodoo Authentica and does tarot card readings in Jackson Square, but is probably best known as the most visible elder in the New Orleans Vampire Association.

Maven Lore (again, somehow that feels . . .) is another elder and locally renowned as New Orleans' premier fangsmith. A fangsmith is someone who specializes in the art of making custom fangs for members of the vampire community as well as others who may want them. Maven's business, Dark Awakenings Custom Fangs, was founded in 1998 and has made fangs for everyone from UFC fighters and exotic dancers to once-a-year fang wearers on Halloween.

NOVA elder Jezabel DeLuna is a pranic vampire, meaning she feeds off of sexual energy, not blood. She holds a PhD in metaphysics and works storefronts on Decatur Street in the French Quarter, selling wine, absinthe, and other spirits. Approaching Halloween each year, she helps host the Anne Rice Ball and Vampire Convention.

With all the many haunted bars in New Orleans, of course one bar is the hangout for vampires. The Dungeon (738 Toulouse Street) has a foreboding entrance with a narrow, dark, damp alleyway that opens up into a small patio. Inside the bar is dark and does, in fact, feel like a dungeon. The restrooms are hidden behind bookcases for reasons we mortals don't understand. Upstairs has a bar and a mirrored dance floor, which I'm guessing doesn't show the reflections of many dancers, and a real coffin hanging overhead from the ceiling. Rock, punk, and techno tunes, which you should know were the preferred music styles of vampires if you've seen *Lost Boys*, *Buffy*, or *Vampire Academy*, blast at a volume that could, and perhaps does, wake the dead.

Please note: No photos are allowed inside the Dungeon. I think the owner wants to maintain an air of mystery.

Lastly, when there is an online dating service for people over 60 and another just for farmers, there's got to be some for vampires. I found two. One group, www.vampirepassions.com, bills itself as a 100 percent free online dating and social networking site for vampires and vampire lovers. Browse the vampire groups to find members based on whether you are into sanguine vampirism or psychic vampirism. The site makes connections based on blood type. The other, www.datevampires.com, claims to be the largest single vampire community and has tons of active profiles posted by members. "Are you a vampire chick looking for a man that you can sink your teeth into? This culture is taking the web by storm and we make it easy for you to find others that share the same dark passions. It's not just a fetish, it's a lifestyle; so, come and find your vampire lover today."

CHAPTER 4

Hooray for Horrorwood

This was New Orleans, a magical and magnificent place to live. In which a vampire, richly dressed and gracefully walking through the pools of light of one gas lamp after another might attract no more notice in the evening than hundreds of other exotic creatures. —**Anne Rice**

To me, vampires are sex . . . I don't get a vampire story about abstinence. I'm 53. I don't care about high school students. I find them irritating and uninformed. —**Alan Ball, creator of *True Blood***

Y ou may or may not believe there are real vampires, but there can be no doubt about reel vampires and their huge impact upon New Orleans.

According to FilmLA, a private, nonprofit organization established to coordinate permits for on-location movies, TV shows, and commercials, Hollywood is no longer the film capital of America. Over the last 15 years, California has dropped from 64 percent of all film locations to 8 percent, and 2013 was the first year a city other than Los Angeles and Hollywood played home to the largest number of productions. The new champion is New Orleans.

12 Years a Slave, The Dallas Buyer's Club, Fantastic Four, and *Duck Dynasty* certainly contribute to the stockpile of filmed in New Orleans hits. But at the heart of New Orleans explosion in popularity are vampire films and TV shows. *True Blood, The Originals, Cirque du Freak, Interview with the Vampire,* and others have helped sustain and even grown the image of New Orleans as Vampire Central.

A study on the impact of all these movies revealed that last year alone New Orleans movies contributed 13,700 local jobs and tossed $976 million into the local economy. The study did not take into account television productions, which, with the absence of *True Blood* and *The Originals*, means they left out a lot.

Over three hundred vampire movies have been made by studios, and, if you count independent film companies, this number probably climbs well into the thousands. Over one thousand vampire novels have been published in last 25 years. With the success of Stephenie Meyer's Twilight series, both as books and films, vampire romance has become a new and hugely popular sub-genre.

Any discussion of New Orleans vampire books and films has to start with Anne Rice. Probably every bit as much as the strip clubs on Bourbon Street or crawfish boils and po'boys, her novels served to draw visitors to New Orleans, hungry to immerse themselves in Anne's dark world.

Her first novel, *Interview with the Vampire*, published in 1976, was written, in large part, as a way for Anne Rice to deal with the raw feelings surrounding the death of her six-year-old daughter, Michele. Anne told *Publisher's Weekly*:

I got to the point where the whole thing just exploded! Suddenly, in the guise of Louis, a fantasy figure, I was able to touch the reality that was mine. It had something to do with growing up in New Orleans, this strange, decadent city full of antebellum houses. It had something to do with my old-guard Catholic background. It had something to do with the tragic loss of my daughter and with the death of my mother when I was fourteen. Through Louis' eyes, everything became accessible. But I didn't ask when I was writing what it meant; I only asked if it felt authentic. There was an intensity—an intensity that's still there when I write about those characters. As long as it is there, I will go on with them. In some way they are a perfect metaphor for me.

By her second and third vampire novels, *The Vampire Lestat* and *Queen of the Damned*, Anne had become a fixture on top of best-seller lists and had awakened book publishers to the cash cow opportunities offered by vampire

1239 First Street, the former and forever "Anne Rice house"   ALEXEY SERGEEV

novels. *Interview* had been rejected five times before being sold to Knopf (actually not so bad, considering Stephenie Meyer's *Twilight* was rejected 14 times), and even then, Anne received a rather lukewarm advance of $12,000. But, in just a few short years, she had become as big a celebrity as any writer. Fans, many dressed up as vampires, would camp out for her book signings in numbers that were book equivalent of queues waiting for U2 or Rolling Stones concert tickets. Anne thrilled her fans by sometimes showing up for book signings lying inside a quilted coffin in a horse-drawn hearse. At the events, she would sign as many as six thousand books.

Being a celebrity vampire novelist is not without complications. Voyeuristic Goth kids started hanging at the fence of her home at 1239 First Street, hoping to get a glimpse of Anne, or trying to spot the giant oak where the fictional Lasher and Emaleth are imaginarily buried, or to merely breathe in the same rarified jasmine- and sweet olive-infused air Anne breathed, or to stand on the same cracked and broken banquettes (what you call sidewalks) where Anne's feet might have touched the ground on her way from the front gate to her always-waiting vampire limo parked out front. Much to the delight of her fans but chagrin of her neighbors, Anne chose to give free Monday night tours of her home. The line on First Street would stretch to St. Charles.

Then *Interview* was sold for film. She describes her Hollywood experiences as "feasting with panthers—you don't even know till you get home that half your body's been eaten." After years of false starts and her dashed hopes of having actors from Rutger Hauer to Daniel Day Lewis play Lestat, Anne was devastated when the studio chose to cast diminutive boy-next-door Tom Cruise and all-American hunk Brad Pitt as the leads. She took out full-page ads complaining about their choices and hoping to block the film. However, upon seeing the actual movie, she loved it.

Since then, Anne has had several more high-profile in-print debates. There was a very public feud with Al Copeland, eccentric founder of the Popeye's fried chicken chain, who had the audacity to build a garish, neon-splattered restaurant on a site that figured prominently in *Memnoch the Devil*. In full-page ads in the *Times-Picayune*, Anne condemned his lack of aesthetic taste, as though he was defiling a sacred spot. The equally wealthy Al Copeland fired back with lambasting ads of his own, and *it was on*!

When anonymous Amazon reviewers attacked her novel *Blood Canticle*, Rice posted on the site a blistering 1,200-word defense of her book, ripping into the posted critics who, she wrote, were "interrogating this text from the wrong perspective." She kicked it up a notch: "Your stupid, arrogant assumptions about me and what I am doing are slander. You have used the site as if it were a public urinal to publish falsehood and lies." It's a safe bet they won't be invited to next year's Vampire Ball.

Anne left New Orleans in 2002 following the death of her husband, poet-artist Stan Rice. "I was creatively and emotionally exhausted and craving a fresh start," she said. "I guess I wanted to go to a place with no memories and no history, with light pouring in the windows."

Even though Anne hasn't lived at her Garden District home in over a decade, you may still wish to walk by the house on First Street. The front fence plaque (tell me the design in the iron fence doesn't look like little skulls) describes the house as once belonging to both Anne Rice and Albert Hamilton Brevard. The wealthy Brevard brought exotic plants from all over the world. In New Orleans' subtropical climate they all flourished. Later, Brevard went bankrupt and attempted suicide on his front porch. The gunshot to the head was a mortal wound, but did not immediately kill him. While he lay on his deathbed, word spread throughout the neighborhood and his lovely neighbors used the opportunity to dig up Brevard's plants for their own yards. While far from a magnanimous gesture, the acts of the neighbors did contribute greatly to the lushness of the Garden District.

The house went on the market for $3.75 million. I thought this was a steal. I figured the new owner could make back every penny by renting out a few bedrooms as a B&B. Her legions of fans would pay any price to spend a night in the Anne Rice House. But I doubt the Garden District Neighborhood Association would allow this. It currently blocks any tour buses from driving the district's hallowed streets. If you want to see the homes of Sandra Bullock and John Goodman, or where Nicolas Cage and Trent Reznor used to live, or the yard where Peyton and Eli Manning learned to chuck a football, you'll need to do a walking tour. And no littering or gum cracking while walking the streets of the Garden District, or you'll learn there are far worse things awaiting man than death.

If Anne Rice is the queen (now in exile) of the vampire scene in New Orleans, her court includes Poppy Z. Brite, Andrew Fox, and Charlaine Harris.

Poppy Z. Brite, now named Billy Martin after sex reassignment surgery, cut her teeth as a writer of gothic horror novels *Lost Souls*, *Exquisite Corpse*, and *Drawing Blood*. Her vampires were unlike those of traditional lore. Rather than being transformed, undead humans, they are a separate species who were born as vampires. While most feed on blood, some find alternatives, sucking on love and beauty. Poppy's older vampires have fangs, are sensitive to sunlight, and do not eat food or drink . . . wine. Her younger, rebellious vampires have normal human teeth that must be filed down to become jugular piercers so they can eat and drink. Poppy's vampires mostly

Nosferatu ascending the stairs

like Chartreuse, a French liqueur made by Carthusian monks. All of the novels feature gay men as main characters, graphic sexual scenes, and wry treatment of terribly gruesome events.

Andrew Fox has also writes about vampires that play against stereotype. He reasoned that "If vampires actually 'lived' in New Orleans and subsisted on the blood of New Orleanians, they'd be sucking down a stew of cholesterol and fatty lipids with every meal. After a century or so, a New Orleans vampire would look a heck of a lot more like John Goodman than Tom Cruise." Fox created Jules Duchon, the obese vampire protagonist in the novels *Fat White Vampire Blues* and *Bride of the Fat White Vampire*. The fictional Duchon was born and bred in the working-class Ninth Ward and, even after being bitten and becoming a vampire, he kept his job as a cab driver. He could barely fit behind the wheel of his very big Cadillac taxi, even with the seat pushed all the way back.

Miami Beach–born Andrew Fox wrote on his website of his early inspiration,

> When I was seven or so, my father treated me to a drive-in double feature of *The Return of Count Yorga* and *Scream, Blacula, Scream!* All the fangs and blood blew my young mind; either that, or all the polyester leisure suits and gold medallions. I'd beg my parents to buy me any comic book that had a vampire on the cover—whether it was Spider-Man battling Morbius or Jimmy Olsen being menaced by a Hollywood bloodsucker . . . The new crop of vampires—romantic, misunderstood, aristocratic eternals, or gorgeous, savage teens who looked like "heroin chic" jeans models—failed to capture my fancy. I couldn't relate. Maybe I just preferred my vampires the old-fashioned way: dour, dusty, with bad foreign accents and worse attitudes. Lon Chaney, Jr.'s Count Alucard probably most closely approximated my ideal . . . not too handsome, not too graceful, always looking faintly embarrassed as he skulked around.

The novels of Charlaine Harris are the epitome of what failed to capture Fox's fancy. A telepathic waitress working in a rural Louisiana bar and having sex with a vampire, while a whole town of synthetic blood drinking vampires have sex with mortals, a few werewolves, shape-shifters, witches, maenads (frenzied women with booze and boa constrictors), and other vampires—not exactly the old-fashioned way.

If you bumped carts in the local supermarket with Charlaine Harris, born and raised in the Mississippi Delta, you'd have no idea this was the woman who writes hot sex scenes between vampires and mortals, and which have sold 32 million copies. She said in a *New York Times* interview, "Every trip to Wal-Mart is an inspiration." It took Miss Charlaine 30 years of Walmart shopping and writing to become an overnight sensation. The first of her Sookie Stackhouse vampire books sold for only $5,000.

As was the case with Anne Rice, fame and success has its downside.

After 13 Southern Vampire novels, she ended the series with *Dead Ever After*. Some passionate fans were upset that Sookie didn't end up with the vampire they wanted. "I've been getting death threats," Ms. Harris revealed in an interview.

Her great good fortune happened one day when writer-director-producer Alan Ball was early for a dentist appointment. He used his time browsing a nearby Barnes & Noble store, where he picked up one of her novels. This led to his buying the film adaptation rights and creating the HBO series *True Blood*. For one who has not lived even a single lifetime, Alan Ball was a wise man. The TV show averages five million viewers and has won an Emmy, a Golden Globe, and Screen Actors Guild Awards.

It's also been a boon for the town of Clinton, Louisiana. Fifty miles from New Orleans, Clinton claims to be the real-life setting for what's called Bon Temps, Louisiana, in the TV series. Years ago, it was the setting for *Dukes of Hazard*. Most of *True Blood* is shot in the other LA, Los Angeles, but certain scenes and the introductory episodes were filmed in and around Clinton. During filming, traffic had to be routed around Clinton's downtown, creating a nuisance for cross-parish travelers. But the series employed more than 50 local residents, including Audrey Faciane, executive director of the parish's Chamber of Commerce and a parish tourism commissioner. She got a small part as one of the Bon Temps residents turned crazy by Maryann's mood magic. She's now "efforting" an annual True Blood Festival that would bring tourism money to Clinton, maybe with T-shirts making fun of Ted Cruz and Sarah Palin, as did the TV show, and GOD HATES FANGS bumper stickers.

Whereas 2014 was the final season for *True Blood*, *The Originals* is just getting going. The CW Network first aired its vampire series in October 2013. By the time *Fear Dat* creeps onto any bookstore shelves, there may well be one or 10 additional vampire movies or TV series. I wouldn't be surprised if Bravo or the SyFy Channel concocted some vampire reality show.

While the vampire movies made in New Orleans have greatly helped the local economy, other than *Interview with the Vampire*, they have been heaped with neither great praise nor success.

While reviewers were lukecool (38% on Rotten Tomatoes), *Cirque du Freak* did make money for Universal Pictures. The film, based on graphic novels by Darren Shan, yielded $14 million domestically and nearly $40 million worldwide. It was the #1 movie in the Ukraine and #2 in in the United Arab Emirates. And it's always good to see John C. Reilly in anything. A sequel has been threatened.

Dracula 2000 has spawned a three film series, though the two sequels were direct to video releases. The *New York Times* called *Dracula 2000* "a grating new cliché carelessly tossed into a picture to give it a hip kinetic gloss." Its sequel *Dracula II: Ascension* was routinely dismissed as "a tired collection of clichés" (Entertainment Weekly), whereas *Dracula III: Legacy* fared slightly better. For one, it starred the Anne Rice–desired Rutger Hauer as Dracula. One reviewer wrote, "[It's] at least somewhere just north of mediocre."

I actually liked watching *Abraham Lincoln: Vampire Hunter*, but my pleasure came mostly from recognizing local spots used as the movie sets. "Hey, that's the Pharmacy Museum! Isn't that the Jonathan Ferrara Gallery?" The acting and the plot, such as they were, provided decidedly less pleasure.

Marie Laveau, the Voodoo Queen   MOLLY MAGUIRE

CHAPTER 5

Voodoo

New Orleans is unique in the world. This city has a life and a spirit and a soul that's missing in most places. It's all because of the Voodoo perspective there's this invisible reality that's reflected darkly into the physical world, but that invisible reality is full of spirit and life. It's so beautiful and alive underneath our feet. All we have to do is open up to it, recognize it, and bring it through. Our life becomes richer. —**Sallie Ann Glassman, voodoo priestess**

I don't think anyone wants to cuddle a zombie. —**Norman Reedus**

My wife, and others, warned me about writing this chapter. My irreverent (some would say smart ass) tone could get me in trouble. You don't mess with voodoo. Even seasoned ghost hunter Zak "Bilbo" Bagans, of the Travel Channel's *Ghost Adventures*, skedaddled out of Magnolia Lane Plantation when the presenters came upon triple X voodoo signs.

In writing the chapter, I have encountered what others might view as "warning signs." I described one voodoo lady in New Orleans as looking like she just pushed back from the server's counter at KFC, but not before smearing two packets of mayonnaise on her cheeks. When I returned to my laptop, the entire entry had disappeared into the ether. Browser malfunction . . . or voodoo? Our gray cat, fittingly named Gris Gris, went missing. The normal behavior of a once feral cat . . . or voodoo? LeBron James retook his talents back to Cleveland. A smart career choice . . . or voodoo?

In interviewing psychics, ghost hunters, and voodoo practitioners, I chose not to contact voodoo and zombie expert Alyne Pustanio, who's also a Facebook friend. My reason was that among her books is *Risks Incidental: Supernatural Dangers of Paranormal Exploration*. I figured she probably knows stuff or has had experienced stuff I just don't want to hear about while writing this book, for fear of returning my advance to the publisher, deleting all files pertaining to *Fear Dat*, and sprinkling salt at my doors and along my windows.

Countless tourists will fly home from New Orleans with their luggage packed with a packet of Love Potion Number 9 or a keychain with attached small plastic voodoo doll. But in New Orleans voodoo is more than cute consumables. In New Orleans, voodoo is the Real Thing.

Voodoo was first brought here from Africa. Slaves in Louisiana began arriving in 1719. The majority of enslaved Africans came directly from what is now Benin, West Africa, bringing with them their language and religious beliefs rooted in spirit and ancestor worship. In Benin's Fon language, *vodun* means "spirit," an invisible, mysterious force that can intervene in human affairs

One reason voodoo developed here and much less so in the rest of America is largely because the French—then Spanish, then French again—owned Louisiana. They were far more tolerant of the practices and faith of the slave population than were all those Brits who came to America for their own religious freedom but suppressed others'.

Another reason was sheer numbers. According to a census of 1731–1732, the ratio of enslaved African to European settlers in New Orleans was over two to one. The white minority would have been hard pressed to suppress the voodoo faith.

New Orleans–style voodoo evolved like New Orleans–style Creole cuisine, as a blend of different cultures. One of the main different cultures happens to be Catholicism. Some feel the people who practiced voodoo started using Catholic saints, holy water, and the Lord's Prayer in their ceremonies as a mask to hide voodoo in plain sight. Others feel it was a conscious decision by the enslaved to integrate some Catholicism into voodoo because the white man's magic seemed to have some power, being as the white man had the much better deal as slave owner rather than slave. For many, the blending of voodoo with Catholicism was simply a matter of natural evolution. Over many years away from their homeland, slaves slowly lost the thread of their native beliefs and the predominant Catholicism of New Orleans bled into their language and practices.

Marie Laveau herself was a lifetime Catholic. Jerry Gandolfo, owner of the Historic Voodoo Museum, said "Voodoo is the black sister of the Catholic church." Brandi Kelley, owner of Voodoo Authentica, describes her own integrated Catholic-voodoo lifestyle as follows: "On Sunday, I light candles and make offerings to Catholic saints. On other days, I light candles and make offerings to voodoo *loas.*"

Voodoo here grew to be quite a bit different from Haitian Vodou. The evolution of a local style created many new and first time practices we now associate as the basic tenets of voodoo, including gris-gris, voodoo dolls, and, most important, voodoo queens. In Africa voodoo is male-dominated. The opposite grew to be true in New Orleans. The slaves gave credit to a female spirit, Aida Wedo, for allowing them to survive the ocean crossing. Women achieved central importance in New Orleans–style voodoo.

Marie Laveau is far and away the most famous voodoo queen, but she was not the first. Sanite Dede was an earlier practitioner of voodoo in the city. She was a young woman from Santo Domingo who would hold rituals in her courtyard on Dumaine and Chartres Streets, just blocks away from the St. Louis Cathedral. The Times-Picayune printed sensationalized articles about these rituals, telling of "wild and uncontrolled orgies" and "serpent worship."

Annoyed by hearing drumbeats during their Mass and outraged by supposed orgies, the church pushed through an ordinance in 1817 that Catholicism was the only recognized faith in New Orleans, and it became illegal to practice others. Shortly thereafter, the police arrested four hundred women for allegedly dancing naked in Queen Sanite's courtyard.

The unsubstantiated charges were later dropped for lack of evidence. Some Catholics felt voodoo spells either erased the evidence or at least befuddled the minds of prosecutors and judges. But the message was clear, voodoo was not welcomed in New Orleans. Spanish governor Galvez went so far as to place an embargo on importing any slaves from the Caribbean because he worried they were more likely to bring their scary (misunderstood) voodoo practices into his city. Plus, whites worried about too many slaves' having the power to stage a revolt as had occurred in Saint-Domingue. There, 100,000 natives drove out Napoleon's army, abolished slavery, and established the new country of Haiti. To avoid further harassment in New Orleans, voodoo practitioners moved outside the then city limits to swampland on Bayou St. John, near what is now City Park.

The next head of New Orleans voodoo after Sanite Dede was John Montenet, a heavily tattooed voodoo doctor better known as Dr. John. He was a well-respected freeman of color who alternatively said he'd been a prince in Senegal or an African priest. Dr. John had a number of beautiful wives and mistresses, with whom he had over 50 children. Beyond spreading the gospel of his Dr. Johnson, he was famous for predicting the future, casting spells, making gris-gris, and reading minds.

Dr. John was the first in New Orleans to use voodoo for personal profit. He'd charge fees to whip together potions and gris-gris. He reportedly confessed to friends that his magic was faked. "He had been known to laugh," writes Robert Tallant in Voodoo in New Orleans, "when he told of selling a gullible white woman a small jar of starch and water for five dollars."

Dr. John, was later the mentor, instructor, and some even say, the power behind Marie Laveau herself. She eventually decided to break away from Dr. John and set up what could be considered her own practice.

Marie Laveau became for voodoo what Louis Armstrong is for jazz. By that, I mean there are several who claim to have invented jazz. Jelly Roll Morton said, "It is known, beyond contradiction, that New Orleans is the cradle of jazz, and I myself happen to be the inventor." Most music scholars attribute the invention to Buddy Bolden. But it was Louis Armstrong who made jazz internationally famous. Marie Laveau may have followed Sanite Dede and Dr. John, but it was she who made voodoo notorious and everlasting.

Born in New Orleans, maybe in 1794, Marie was the illegitimate daughter of a rich Creole plantation owner, Charles Laveau, and his Haitian slave mistress. She married Jacques Paris who, like her, was a free person of color, but she was soon abandoned or maybe widowed. Dates and facts about people who were not emperors, decorated generals, or founders of artistic movements are not always well documented. About 1825, she began a second, common-law marriage to Christophe de Glapion, another free person of color, with whom she would have 15 children. Yes, 15. I'm surprised she had any time left for readings and conjuring . . . and hairdressing.

Marie was a hairdresser for the affluent ladies of New Orleans and used her position to gather gossip. Some of her clients would talk to her during hair appointments about anything and everything. They would divulge their most personal secrets, just as today where you'll tell your hairdresser, or bartender, or Facebook friends the most intimate details of your life you'd never say to anyone else. Marie Laveau gathered additional information using cooks, maids, and domestics as a network of household informants that could rival any FBI sting operation.

Thereby, her "cold readings," where she appeared to "just know" all the little secrets of so many people, were far from her using her psychic or intuitive gifts alone. Her reputation skyrocketed. To visit Marie for a reading became the fashion craze throughout New Orleans, and often with the city's most well-heeled residents. Politicians would pay her as much as $1,000 for her help in winning elections. Uptowners paid $10 (a lot back then) for a simple love potion. Rather than providing straight-up cash payments, judges would often make rulings in ways she desired in order to keep her from revealing the things she "just knew" about them. Marie developed great power.

Above and beyond being a great networker, Marie Laveau had P.T. Barnum showmanship. She knew how to pull in the white man's dollars to see her staged rituals. "Simulated orgies" gets 'em every time. Men and women danced in abandonment after drinking rum and seeming to become possessed by various *loas*. Seated on her throne, Marie directed the action. She kept a large snake called Le Grand Zombi that she would dance with in veneration of Damballah. She would shake a gourd rattle to summon the snake deity, repeating over and over, "Damballah, ye-ye-ye!"

Once a year Marie presided over the ritual of St. John's Eve. It begins at dusk on June 23 and ends at dawn on the next day. St. John's is the most sacred of holy days in the voodoo faith. Hundreds attended her ritual, including white reporters and curious white onlookers, each of whom was charged a sizable fee. Drum beating, bonfires, animal sacrifice, and nude women dancing seductively were all a part of the extended, all-night ritual.

Magnolia bridge   BRANDON PIPER

Except for the nude dancing and the animal sacrifice and the bonfires, this practice on St. John's Eve still takes place today (basically just the drum beating remains). You can join Sallie Ann Glassman and La Source Ancienne Ounfo to celebrate St. John's Eve with the annual head-washing ceremony, a form of voodoo baptism. Come to the Magnolia pedestrian bridge crossing Bayou St. John, near Cabrini High. You are asked to wear all white and

BLACK MAGIC AS TOLD BY A White Guy

In the creation of New Orleans's image as a unique, exotic, sultry seductress that draws nine million visitors a year, Louis Armstrong, Tennessee Williams, Marie Laveau, Paul Prudhomme, and Blaze Starr all had a huge hand (or in the case of Blaze, other body parts), but no one more so than the lesser-known, unassuming Lafcadio Hearn.

This scrawny, bug-eyed, hook-nosed, weak chinned, birdlike figure—born in Greece, raised in Ireland—immigrated to Cincinnati, where he began writing travel pieces for the *Cincinnati Enquirer*—then moved to New Orleans in 1877 and spent 10 very impressionable years here. He'd been fired from the Cincinnati paper for marrying an African American woman, which at the time was a violation Ohio's antimiscegenation law.

Hearn moved to New Orleans and began writings for national publications, such as *Harper's Weekly* and *Scribner's Magazine*. His pieces created the popular reputation of New Orleans as a place with a distinct culture more akin to that of Europe and the Caribbean than to the rest of North America. And he issued some great quotations:

It's not an easy thing to describe one's first impression of New Orleans; for while it actually resembles no other city upon the face of the earth, yet it recalls vague memories of a hundred cities. It owns suggestions of towns in Italy and in Spain, of cities in England and in Germany, of seaports in the Mediterranean, and of seaports in the tropics. I fancy that the power of fascination which New Orleans

exercises upon foreigners is due no less to this peculiar characteristic than to the tropical beauty of the city itself. Whensoever the traveler may have come, he may find in the Crescent City some memory of his home—some remembrance of something he loves.

As a fellow ex-Ohioan, this is perhaps my favorite:

Times are not good here. The city is crumbling into ashes. It has been buried under taxes and frauds and maladministrations so that it has become a study for archaeologists . . . but it is better to live here in sackcloth and ashes than to own the whole state of Ohio.

So, for all the good he did in helping make New Orleans a tourist destination, I will try to forgive him for also helping (greatly) to create the largely false and enduring image of voodoo as a pagan ritual built around snake handling, bourbon drinking, nude dancing, and sticking pins into voodoo dolls, with the occasional biting the head off a chicken. Not that there's anything wrong with any of that.

In his article called "New Orleans Superstitions" that originally appeared in *Harper's Weekly* Christmas Day 1886, he wrote a detailed description of voodoo practices:

The fear of what are styled "Voudoo charms" is much more widely spread in Louisiana than any one who had conversed only with educated residents might suppose; and the most familiar superstition of this class is the belief in

Lafcadio Hearn

spite of fetiches; but the surest way to provide against being "hoodooed," as American residents call it, is to open one's pillow from time to time. If any charms are found, they must be first sprinkled with salt, then burned.

Scattering dirt before a door, or making certain figures on the wall of a house with chalk, or crumbling dry leaves with the fingers and scattering the fragments before a residence, are also forms of a maleficent conjuring which sometimes cause serious annoyance.

A negro charm to retain the affections of a lover consists in tying up the legs of the bird to the head, and plunging the creature alive into a vessel of gin or other spirits.

Tearing the live bird asunder is another cruel charm, by which some negroes believe that a sweetheart may become magically fettered to the man who performs the quartering.

Here, as in other parts of the world, the crowing hen is killed, the hooting of the owl presages death or bad luck, and the crowing of the cock by day presages the arrival of company.

It is dangerous to throw hair-combings away instead of burning them, because birds may weave them into their nests and while the nest remains the person to whom the hair belonged will have a continual headache.

what I might call pillow magic, which is the supposed art of causing wasting sicknesses or even death by putting certain objects into the pillow of the bed in which the hated person sleeps. Feather pillows are supposed to be particularly well adapted to this kind of witchcraft. It is believed that by secret spells a "Voudoo" can cause some monstrous kind of bird or nondescript animal to shape itself into being out of the pillow feathers—like the tupilek of the Esquimau iliseenek (witchcraft). It grows very slowly, and by night only; but when completely formed, the person who has been using the pillow dies.

Putting an open pair of scissors under the pillow before going to bed is supposed to insure a pleasant sleep in

VOODOO

It is bad luck to move a cat from one house to another; seven years' bad luck to kill a cat; and the girl who steps, accidentally or otherwise, on a cat's tail need not expect to be married the same year.

The apparition of a white butterfly means good news.

The neighing of a horse before one's door is bad luck.

When a fly bothers one very persistently, one may expect to meet an acquaintance who has been absent many years.

The red-fish has the print of St. Peter's fingers on its tail.

If water won't boil in the kettle, there may be a toad or a toad's egg in it.

Never kill a spider in the afternoon or evening, but always kill the spider unlucky enough to show himself early in the morning.

If you are bewitched, boil a beef heart and while it is cooking, keep sticking it with a needle; the witch will have the same pains, and the spell upon you will be broken.

If you think someone is doing you harm, get a two prong fork and go to a crossroad where they walk, and bury it [prongs up] so they will walk over it, using their name [abusing their name; cursing them] while you are burying it, and say, "In the Name of the Father, Son and Holy Ghost," and they will swell up and just pop open and die.

To overcome a hoodoo, kill a lizard. Do it by smoking. Beat it to a powder. Mix the powder with whiskey. Drink it. This will cure you.

If someone is bothering you and you don't want them to, you take a handful of salt and call their name and throw it over your right shoulder and they will not bother you.

If you think you are hoodooed, take one pint of salt, one pint of corn meal, one pint of your urine. Put that in a can on the stove at twelve o'clock at night and cook until it burns. Then throw the can and all away and your hoodoo spell will be off.

Except for the part about toad eggs and cooking a pint of your own urine, most of this sounds just made up to me. Maybe all these "facts" were created by a couple of Creoles pulling Lafcadio's scrawny leg.

bring a white scarf or rag for your head. Though, as one spiritualist pointed out to me, "It looks a little suspect when it's all white people dressed in all white that come to participate in a ritual based on an Afro-Caribbean faith."

Marie Laveau herself had dual identities. While her image invokes fear in some, others feel she is worthy of sainthood. Where she charged politicians and uptown ladies hefty fees, she provided many services for free when she attended to the sick during the outbreak of yellow fever, ministered to prisoners on death row, or helped others in need who simply had no money. Still . . . I will stick with my advice in chapter 2, that you should leave Marie something if you visit her grave.

After Marie Laveau's death, a second Marie Laveau (her daughter) the new queenpin of New Orleans voodoo. Undoubtedly, having the same name led to confusion and added to her aura. There is additionally the fact that Marie Laveau, the daughter, was born when Marie Laveau, the mother, was only 14 years old. It's not hard to see how an aura was established by her seemingly being in two places at once, or being timelessly youthful, or being seen at rituals after her death. There literally were two Marie Laveaus.

During the 1930s, true voodoo went underground again. Tourism had become the foundation of the New Orleans economy. City leaders didn't want to frighten off tourists with the completely sensationalized image of voodoo as created in Hollywood by movies, such as the 1932 *White Zombie* and later *I Walked with a Zombie*, and best-selling books like *Magic Island* by W. B. Seabrook. The Roman Catholic Church continued its decades-old campaign to present Catholicism as the legitimate religion and voodoo as pagan heresy.

It was during this time that Fred Staten was born and would live his entire life in New Orleans. Frank reinvented himself as "Prince Keeyama," a voodoo man. Keeyama would tell outlandish tales. He claimed to be a native of Port-au-Prince, Haiti. He claimed his brother was the Haitian prime minister, and that they were both raised by Papa Doc Duvalier. Keeyama told these stories without the slightest hint of a Haitian accent. He bragged of his expertise with snakes, yet couldn't answer the most basic questions about the different types of snakes. He took credit for training two lions at the zoo, although the zoo has no such knowledge or records.

Rather than his being a genuine voodoo man, most considered him a genuine voodoo nightclub act. His performances consisted of eating fire, handling snakes, and sticking needles through his throat. But it was the finale that made Prince Keeyama a local legend. He would pretend to place a chicken in a trance, then bite off its head and drink the blood. He then ripped open the breast and ate raw chicken meat. That he never got Salmonella poisoning may attest to his powers.

Known to everyone as "Chicken Man," Keeyama was entertaining in an over-the-top Andy Kaufman or Lady Gaga kind of way. He was generally beloved as a French Quarter character, but few took him seriously as a voodooist. He was deliberately not invited to participate in a Tulane University panel discussion on voodoo in the mid-'70s. As years went on, Prince Keeyama was often found wandering the French Quarter in his voodoo attire, selling voodoo dolls and gris-gris bags, but he had abandoned his signature act. Chicken Man admitted "I got tired biting chicken heads. It got kinda funky." He briefly had a shop called Chicken Man's House of Voodoo, located on Bourbon Street. Fred Staten died in December 1998. His ashes were donated to the Voodoo Spiritual Temple.

Voodoo today is making something of a comeback in two practically opposite directions. There's the touristy voodoo rebirth, where voodoo shops selling made-in-China gris-gris bags and pin dolls are about as common as nail salons. You can even pick up your voodoo candles at Zuppardo's Grocery along with your instant grits and frozen burritos. Wherever Marie Laveau is buried, she must be rolling over in her grave with new voodoo products like Go Away Evil air freshener and Shut Your Mouth mouthwash. You can have your picture taken with the Voodoo Couple or the Voodoo Man, people who wander the French Quarter on sunny days, hoping to get cash tips for posing in front of tourist's cameras. You can pay a for-hire voodoo doctor or queen to attend your next party or function.

At this same time, "something very real is happening," said Martha Ward, a professor of anthropology at the University of New Orleans. "Americans today are hungry for spiritual fulfillment, and voodoo offers a direct experience with the sacred that appeals to more and more people. This is especially visible in New Orleans, which has always been a center of these beliefs." Ina Fandrich, the author of a Marie Laveau biography and professor of religion at Louisiana State University, called the growth in voodoo beliefs "enormous. Especially since 9/11, people have been grasping for meaning and guidance," Ms. Fandrich said. "An amazing number of people are finding it in voodoo."

The main focus of Louisiana voodoo today is to serve others and influence the outcome of life events through the connection with nature, spirits, and ancestors. Many "real" rituals are often held behind closed doors. Showy public ritual would be considered disrespectful to the spirits. Voodoo methods include readings, spiritual baths, specially devised diets, prayer, and personal ceremony. Voodoo is often used to cure anxiety, addictions, depression, loneliness, and other ailments. It seeks to help the hungry, the poor, and the sick just as Marie Laveau once did.

The appeal of voodoo now cuts across racial and national lines. Even the Catholic Church has jumped onboard. During the Second Vatican Council of the 1960s, the Catholic Church recognized African traditional religions as accepted forms of spirituality. Pope John Paul II attended voodoo ceremonies in Togo in 1985 and Benin in 1993 and helped lift the veil of mystery and misunderstanding. Though not completely. The Archdiocese of New Orleans is not on board. If you visit Marie Laveau's grave, notice the wording on her plaque says she practiced the voodoo "cult" and not "faith."

Just as certain people cling to the belief that Obama is from Nigeria and Elvis is still alive, some view all voodoo as hokum, yet are still a little afraid of the voodoo faith.

The book *Voodoo & Hoodoo* was banned in Slidell Junior High because it included recipes for spells. Texas banned Dixie Beer from transporting a new product, Blackened Voodoo Lager, across its god-fearing (or rather voodoo fearing) state lines. I can't imagine any believers in voodoo squealed with delight as they watched their faith reduced to the cartoon character Dr. Facilier, the villain in Disney's *The Princess and the Frog*. Do you think if George H. W. Bush had used the term *Hasidic economics* or *Baptist economics*, it would have been so quickly and universally adopted as meaning "screwy or fraudulent economics"?

But the Reverend Pat Robertson takes the cake. After the earthquake in Haiti, he took to the airwaves to say Haitians deserved all the death and destruction because, in following voodoo, they "swore a pact with the devil."

If I had any skills in voodoo, which I do not, or if I was a legitimate member of the voodoo faith, rather than a culture-dipping interloper, I'd put a hex of Pat Robertson. I might toss Dennis Hastert into the stew as well for his offensive remarks right after Hurricane Katrina that New Orleans should just be bulldozed over. But then, I've seen Adelia Elmer, a.k.a. "Dede," Pat Robertson's wife. To wake up to that each morning is much worse than anything I could conjure.

Miss Hope of French Quarter Phantom Tours

CHAPTER 6

Ghosts

I wouldn't touch New Orleans with a ten-foot pole. That town is haunted as shit, and all the better for it. Nowhere in the world loves its ghosts more than that city. —**Kendare Blake**

Seeing a ghost in New Orleans is as common as having a bowl of gumbo. The question is not when, but where best to savor them both. —**Kala Ambrose**

When I wrote *Eat Dat*, about New Orleans' food culture, one of my biggest issues was which of our 1,389 restaurants to include in the book and which to leave out. The same is true here. We have too many ghosts to mention all of them in one book, let alone a single chapter. The International Society for Paranormal Research (ISPR), sort of the FCC of psychic foundations, has documented at least 27 areas of paranormal activity in New Orleans. If you believe ghost tour guides, you can triple or quadruple that number.

Even our most sacred spots are haunted by spirits. Père Antoine was formerly a priest at the St. Louis Cathedral, one of the oldest Catholic churches in America. His body is buried within the church, but his ghost is still hanging around, sometimes seen taking early morning strolls in the ally alongside the church. He is reliably spotted by parishioners and tourists holding a candle and singing slightly off key each year at the Christmas Midnight Mass.

Here I've chosen just five ghost stories representing a wide range of aw-c'mon-ness (the level of "Aw, c'mon!" reaction of disbelief each story will engender). I have no doubt some will be upset that I left out the story of the Octoroon Mistress. It's one of our most famous, but (for me) it lacks a certain gruesomeness. The LaLaurie Mansion and Gardette-LePretre House, however, have plenty of dead and hacked-up bodies. Their tales must be true because there are documented police reports and the police would never lie.

Well, there was that *one* time. Police found a dead body on Tchoupitoulas. This was back in the day when policemen had to handwrite five copies of each report. Rather than writing "Tchoupitoulas" five times, they dragged the body to Camp Street.

The Lady Brandishes

Our most famous haunted house is, without question, The LaLaurie Mansion (1140 Royal Street in the French Quarter). Madame Delphine LaLaurie, a New Orleans socialite, and her husband, Dr. Lou, both had colossal sadistic streaks. In public they were a well-respected couple. But behind the closed doors of their home, they exercised whatever wretched impulse popped into their sick little minds. Madame LaLaurie is said to have killed over 70 slaves, and in the most horrific ways. Her first known victim was a 12-year-old girl who fell to her death from a balcony while trying to run away from her bullwhip-wielding mistress. They tried to secretly bury her body in an old well in the rear courtyard. However, once discovered, charges of abuse were brought upon Delphine LaLaurie. This was

LaLaurie Mansion   ALEXEY SERGEEV

one of several charges that had been placed upon her for abusing slaves. The court issued a fine of only $300, even by 1800s standards a mere slap on the wrist. Her slaves however, were taken away and sold at public auction. The couple got a friend to buy all the slaves and then give them back to the LaLauries.

Then, the LaLauries, as Emeril might say, kicked it up a notch. They chained slaves to the wall to perform experiments. The house cook, also a slave, purposefully set a fire on April 10, 1834, so firemen would enter the mansion and discover the LaLauries' horrendous hobbies. According to Jeanne deLavigne's book *Ghost Stories of Old New Orleans* (written in 1946), the responding firemen found "male slaves, stark naked, chained to the wall, their eyes gouged out, their fingernails pulled off by the roots; others had their joints skinned and festering, great holes in their buttocks where the flesh had been sliced away, their ears hanging by shreds, their lips sewn together . . . Intestines were pulled out and knotted around naked waists. There were holes in skulls, where a rough stick had been inserted to stir the brains." *Journey into Darkness: Ghosts and Vampires of New Orleans* (written 52 years later in 1998), by Kalila Katherina Smith, added more explicit details, including a "victim [who] obviously had her arms amputated and her skin peeled off in a circular pattern, making her look like a human caterpillar," and another who had had her limbs broken and reset "at odd angles so she resembled a human crab."

The story gets more embellished and deeply disgusting with each retelling, and it gets retold about 20 times a night by a continuous parade of ghost tour guides. It's kind of like how the older I get, my high school football exploits become more and more filled with last second heroics. Give me another year or two and my football career and Peyton Manning's will be indistinguishable.

Since *Fear Dat* is the most recent book to write about the LaLaurie Mansion, let me add that one room inside their house had the walls decorated in a skull pattern made from human blood and excrement, and during Mardi Gras season the LaLauries used human intestines as balcony garlands. This is not the least bit true today, but give it a few years.

After being outed by the fireman as "bat-shit crazy" (that could have been the actual description in the police report), the entire neighborhood gathered to storm the house. The LaLauries escaped by carriage just ahead of the mob and took a schooner along St. John's Bayou to St. Tammany Parish. One rumor is they fled to Paris. Another persists that they lived on the Northshore. There is said to be a tombstone for Madame LaLaurie in St. Louis #1. I have never found any such tombstone, but happy hunting.

Since their departure, the house has had a series of owners, often very briefly, and many ghost sightings. In 1837 the house was completely rebuilt inside. It kind of had to be done, what with the infestation of bodies shoved in the walls and under the floorboards. But then strange stories begin about ghostly sightings, unusual noises, and flickering lights in the upstairs windows. The first new owner only lived in the house for three months. The house was then rented out as a furniture store. That, too, quickly vacated after the furniture kept losing resell value, having been mysteriously and repeatedly covered in a foul liquid filth. The owner suspected vandals and waited one night with a shotgun, hoping to catch them in the act. When dawn came, he'd seen nothing but the furniture was once again ruined in stanky goo. He closed the place down shortly thereafter.

The mansion has since housed a girl's school, a conservatory for music, a refuge for young delinquents, home of the Grand Consistory of Louisiana (a Scottish Kite of Freemasonry), and an apartment building in which one tenant, Joseph Edouard Vigne, was found dead upstairs behind his door that mysteriously had been draped in black crepe by someone or something. A bar named the Haunted Saloon tried to take advantage of the building's ghost tales, but patrons stayed away in droves. Its most famous owner has been actor Nicolas Cage. The LaLaurie Mansion belonged to him for several years but allegedly never spent a single night there. However, Sidney Smith, owner of Haunted History Tours, shared with me a humorous anecdote. One night, one of its tour guides was retelling the nasty tales at the front of the mansion. When the guide told the gathered tourists that Nicolas Cage owned the house but never dared to spend the night there, the formerly hidden actor leaned over from the upstairs balcony and yelled down to the crowd, "Oh yeah? Well, I'm here tonight!"

Following Cage, Johnny Depp was rumored to be purchasing the mansion and intending to turn it into a museum. That would have been great on so many levels, but it was actually bought by a man named Michael Whalen. Whalen hired interior decorator Katie Stassi-Scott to redo the inside. Even though she grew up in New Orleans, the now Houston-based interior designer had never heard the horrible tales of Madame LaLaurie. "He told me it was called the LaLaurie house, so I wrote it down and went to Barnes & Noble," said Stassi-Scott. "I asked if they had any books about it, and they said, 'Just look in the haunted house section.'" She was now concerned about her latest gig. "I do believe in good and bad spirits," she said. "I was pregnant at the time, so I went to St. Michael's Church in Houston and got a bottle of holy water. Every time I went to LaLaurie, I would say my prayers and put on the holy water. It was my perfume."

All the Sultan's Whores and All the Sultan's Men Couldn't Put Them Back Together Again

A rental car company, I believe it was Avis, used to have the slogan "We're number two, but we try harder." With the LaLaurie Mansion in town, all others fight for the second-most-haunted spot. The Gardette-LePretre House tries hard to secure that position. Jean Baptiste LePretre owned the house at 716 Dauphine Street. On the outside, it's a pretty typical wrought iron laced balcony, courtyard out back, stunningly beautiful French Quarter mansion. Nothing on the outside betrays the grisly things that took place inside.

Jean Baptiste wanted to rent out his home for the long stretches when he was not in town, living hours outside the city on his plantation. The younger brother of Turkish sultan Prince Suleyman rented the property, then moved in with a complete of entourage of harem girls and his loyal eunuch. I guess in those days would-be tenants didn't have to fill out forms stating how many would occupy the apartment. An answer of "48 and a eunuch" would have raised a few questions.

Once inside the house, the not-quite- sultan held lavish all night absinthe and opium parties. The streets smelled of incense and wild music

LePretre House

was heard till dawn. (Replace wild music with bad covers of '80s hits and substitute incense for the smell of vomit and urine and the LePretre House really wasn't so different from Bourbon Street of today.)

Some say what happened next was because the brother had come to New Orleans with money and jewels stolen from his sibling. Others say it was a hired execution by Suleyman, who would remain the sultan only so long as he was alive. If he died, his younger brother could assume his throne. You know what they say about an ounce of prevention.

One morning a neighbor was strolling down the sidewalk and noticed a large amount of blood running out of the house onto the street. When the police went inside they discovered what was left of everyone from last night's bacchanalia. It was a Charles Manson, *Helter Skelter* scene times six. All 48 occupants had been so thoroughly chopped up and dismembered, police couldn't identify what piece went with whom. The prince had not been hacked to pieces like his entourage. He was found to have been buried alive out back in the courtyard.

It's hard to imagine 48 people would have waited patiently in line while two or three swordsmen sliced and diced a few partygoers at a time. So, there must have been a small army of killers. As densely populated as the French Quarter was and is, to pull this off and not be noticed, we can assume these were professional-grade assassins.

The case has never been solved.

The Gardette-LePretre House is now one of the most haunted places in New Orleans. Witnesses say they have seen the ghosts, heard screams and music, and smelled incense coming from the house.

What's Up, Doc?

Today you can visit the Pharmacy Museum, or "La Pharmacie Française" (514 Chartres Street), the largest and most diverse pharmaceutical collection in the United States. For five dollars, you can see display cases containing artifacts of historical medicinal practices: pills and powders with their original packaging, early and massively cringe-worthy hypodermic needles, tools for therapeutic bloodletting, including a jar labeled "Leeches."

It is the former establishment of Louis J. Dufilho Jr., the first licensed pharmacist in America. He got his license in 1804 and opened this pharmacy in 1823. Monsieur Dufilho and his staff enjoyed a lively business, preparing medicines to fight against yellow fever, dysentery, malaria, and other widespread epidemics of the time. Back then, your pharmacist was basically your family doctor.

The fun begins when Dufilho sold his business to his former employee, Dr. Dupas. Dr. Dupas kept losing his patients. He claimed they were all moving back to France. After he died from syphilis in 1867 (back then, they didn't know syphilis drove you slowly mad), workers found multiple bodies, all believed to be his missing patients, buried in the back courtyard. In addition to murdering his paying customers, Dr. Dupas was revealed to have conducted horrific medical experiments on pregnant slaves.

The brochure for the Pharmacy Museum glosses over these atrocities, scripting, "Visitors are encouraged to walk through the newly renovated courtyard, which contains a garden of herbs used for medicinal purposes in earlier years. The courtyard provides a pastoral, characteristically French Quarter setting for private parties and receptions and is available for rental to large and small groups."

Your private party or reception might have an uninvited guest. Dr. Dupas's apparition has been seen after hours, wearing his brown suit or lab coat. He has been known to throw books and move items in the display cases, and he occasionally sets off the security system. Maybe that's why the NOPD is known for its sluggish response time and moniker "Not Our Problem Darlin'." The police are used to too many false alarms being set off my ghosts.

Yaw and Disorder

The federal building, a city block in size, at 400 Royal Street was a courthouse from 1909 to 1964, then headquarters for the Wildlife and Fisheries Museum, then returned to its role as the Supreme Court of Louisiana in 2004. While undergoing extensive interior renovations to turn a wildlife museum back into a courthouse, the ever busy International Society for Paranormal Research (ISPR) entered the property and discovered several entities.

There's the specter of an African American man who is dressed in a white shirt and pants. A white woman is described as young and is dressed in a brown suit and skirt. Researchers discovered these two were witnesses in a Mafia murder trial in the 1930s. Prior to giving their testimonies, both were shot and killed inside the courtroom. Workers renovating the building and visitors to the courthouse building have also documented witnessing the two witnesses.

The federal building   GEORGE KUCHLER

A third ghost is a man dressed in shirt and tie. According to ISPR, he wanders about the interior of the building and sometimes at night he stands in front of a third-floor window that faces the Omni Hotel across the street. Hotel guests have often reported sightings of this apparition to the staff.

While filming *JFK* inside the building, Oliver Stone is rumored to have shot scenes over and over again as unwanted and no-longer-living extras kept showing up in the dailies.

It Ain't the Meat, It's the Waning Devotion

Back in the 1800s, a young German couple opened a sausage factory in New Orleans. (Okay, you can probably guess the rest of the story on that sentence alone.) The two were well respected in the neighborhood, hardworking and friendly. They'd greet everyone with a smile, and addressed their regular customers by name as they walked in the door. But looks can be deceiving. Once the butcher shop doors were closed and the bloody aprons put away, the husband was getting tired of his wife. He'd married her for better or worse, but not for deboning and filleting. He found a young mistress and fell in love with her.

In order to pursue his new young love, the old meat hacking wife had to go. So, one night after the shop closed, the man crept up behind his wife as she swept the floor, wrapped a cord around her neck, and strangled her.

To dispose of her body, he stuck her headfirst into the sausage grinder. It wasn't a masterfully conceived plan. As the days and weeks passed, he had a harder time fumbling for reasons when customers walked into his shop and asked where his wife was. Saying she was ill, then visiting relatives, he would have eventually escalated to "abducted by aliens" if much more time elapsed.

Gradually, the sausage maker's appearance grew more and more unkempt and haggard. He was barely sleeping, haunted by nightmares of his hacked-up honey's crawling out of the meat grinder to seek revenge.

And then came incidents of customers biting into bits of hair or torn fabric in their breakfast sausage. One day a customer found the wife's gold wedding ring in the sausage. The police were notified and raided the sausage factory that evening. They found the sausage maker huddled in a corner, screaming uncontrollably that his wife was coming to get him. They locked him up in the insane asylum. Inside the asylum, he screamed day and night that his wife's ghost had entered the room. He eventually had a complete mental breakdown and committed suicide.

WHERE TO STAY

In writing this book, I have talked to people far more knowledgeable about ghosts than I am. That'd be like every third person in New Orleans. Most have told me that hotels, restaurants, and bars are the best places to catch sight of a ghost because in their former life, these places of food, drink, and fooling around had the most emotional attachment. Again, I will mention some, but far from all. Phone numbers have been provided for hotels and restaurants in case you want to make reservations.

The Hotel Monteleone
214 Royal St.
(504) 523-3341

The Hotel Monteleone is one of the last, great family-owned hotels in America, having been operated by four generations of the Monteleone family since it was founded in 1886. Tennessee Williams, William Faulkner, and Truman Capote have all lived at the hotel. Truman told people he was born in the hotel, whereas the facts may be otherwise. Eudora Welty was a frequent guest. These residents prompted the Friends of Libraries organization to designate the Monteleone a Literary Landmark. The Hotel

Monteleone is also home to more than a dozen ghosts who have chosen not to check out.

For years, still-living employees and guests of the hotel have reported sightings, as well as ghosts' opening doors, moving soap, and running up charges at checkout by cleaning out the honor bar. (Okay, I made up that last part, but not the rest.) In March 2003, the ISPR spent several days investigating Hotel Monteleone. While at the hotel, the team made contact with enough entities to fill out the cast for a David Simon series. Among them was a man named William Wildemere who'd died inside the hotel of natural causes, the ghost of a jazz singer, a naked man in a feathered Mardi Gras mask (there's always one in every crowd), and a boy who was much older when he died but enjoys returning to Hotel Monteleone as a 10-year-old to play hide-and-seek with another young spirit.

I didn't know you could choose to come back as a ghost a different age than the time of your death. I definitely want to return as myself from days of more hair, less girth, and better knees.

The Cornstalk Hotel
915 Royal St.
(504) 523-1515

The Cornstalk Hotel is a charmer of an old French Quarter hotel with the namesake wrought-iron fence shaped to look like a row of corn, chandeliers in the bedrooms, and a great second-floor balcony from which you can look down on people strolling Royal Street, listen to boats on the Mississippi, and watch bats flutter overhead. It was built in the early 1800s and was the home of Judge François-Xavier Martin, first chief justice of the Louisiana Supreme Court. The hotel also housed Harriet Beecher Stowe, during which time she was inspired by the sights at the nearby slave markets to write *Uncle Tom's Cabin*. But it's listed here because it's also haunted as hell. Reported activity includes the sounds of children running, playing, and laughing, and light footsteps in the halls when no one is there. But the best and one of the creepiest things I've ever heard are tales of guests' staying alone in a room and waking up the next day to discover photos of themselves on their cameras or cell phones, taken while they slept in the room's bed, and taken from the ceiling. Polterazzies?

Hotel Maison de Ville

727 Toulouse St.
(504) 561-5858

You can listen to many types of music in New Orleans: jazz, blues, Cajun, zydeco, bounce, brass band . . . it was even once the opera capital of America. But country is nearly impossible to find, except in Cottage #4 at the Maison de Ville.

Cottage #4 is not located in the main part of the hotel. All cottages are just around the corner on Dauphine Street.

About 20 years ago, the Garth Brooks era, a hotel employee opened the door to Cottage #4 and saw a man dressed in full military uniform and blasting country tunes. The man quickly disappeared, but has been seen since. And every time a maid sets the room radio to a classical station or WWOZ, it gets flipped back to country and the volume is cranked up.

Wonder what this ghost thinks about Big & Rich.

1891 Castle Inn of New Orleans

1539 Fourth St.
(888) 826-0540

Located in the beautiful Garden District, within easy walking distance to St. Charles streetcar, this is most definitely not where you want to stay if you have an important morning meeting. The hotel's own website boasts comments from guests who couldn't get a wink of sleep because of ghosts in their room.

The main culprit is called the "translucent man" because he is often seen in mirrors or briefly seen out of the corner of guest's eyes. He was a servant who died in a fire started by smoking in bed. In life, he spoke several languages, loved the ladies and music, and was a heavy drinker and a smoker. In death, he's quite the prankster. He plays with the radios, televisions, ceiling fans, and lights. His ghost enjoys moving objects to different locations or hiding them. One of the guests couldn't find receipts collected during his trip after he put them in his wallet. His wife eventually found them all in the microwave.

The second known ghost is a little girl who drowned in the pond behind the house. At the time, she was wearing a white dress and was barefoot. Her ghost wanders in the same outfit. She likes to turn water on and off, touches female guests on the leg (as if brushed by a cat), and, like all kids, she loves jumping on the beds.

Le Pavillon Hotel
833 Poydras St.
(800) 535-9095

After former lives as a railroad station and a huge performance hall where circuses performed, a luxury hotel, nicknamed "The Belle of New Orleans," was built on the same spot in 1907. It now displays old-style charm with crystal chandeliers from Czechoslovakia, French marble floors and marble railings, imported from the lobby of the Parisian Grand Hotel, and spectacular Italian columns and statues were bought to add drama to the front entrance.

Le Pavillon Hotel

If you can expense your stay on the company, or you are filthy rich, you should request Palace Suite 730—not for the ghosts, but for the marble bathtub once owned by Napoleon Bonaparte. It's one of only three in the world. One sits in the Louvre. One is in a private collection. And the third is ready to receive you and your suitcase-packed rubber ducky.

What was not imported, but just showed up, are the many ghosts. Paranormal investigation groups line up to conduct research in the hotel. One group got documentation on over a hundred entities and various "haunted hot-spots." Another investigation group found so much activity inside Le Pavilion, they concluded the hotel is portal to the other side.

The most regularly spotted ghost is Adda. The teenaged girl was reportedly set to board a ship with her family when she was killed by a runaway carriage. The hotel staff sees her ghost frequently shuffling around the lobby, often crying, dressed in a flowing ankle-length skirt, a long black shawl, and a broad black hat. More than once she's literally bumped into guests, saying "Pardon me, I am . . . very lost." Before they can ask her where she was headed, Adda disappears.

One New Orleans taxicab driver tells this story over and over again. He swears she got into his cab one cold, rainy night, and asked to be taken to the ship passenger terminal. After he'd driven only a few blocks from the hotel down Poydras Street, she simply disappeared from the backseat into thin air. Said the driver, "I thought she was a real person, I saw her face-to-face and in my rearview mirror. The doorman actually opened the door for her. I drove straight back told him what happened. The doorman shrugged, and said to me. 'Well, this has happened a lot to other cab drivers,' and I am not the first to have taken the ghost girl for a ride."

Other guests report encounters with an aristocratic middle-aged couple. They appear often enough, usually on the second, third, or fourth floor, dressed in dark clothes that seem to be from the 1920s. Room 221 seems to have been the setting for their tryst. The couple are most often holding hands and walking slowly into the elevators. The man smokes a cigar and the pungent smell of smoke lingers in the air. The lady wears a long light blue dress and carries a long, beaded purse. She is said is not to be his wife, but a ghost mistress. How anyone can claim knowledge of an afterlife affair, I have no idea.

Throughout the hotel, guests have heard strange noises and some say they have seen ghosts sit on their beds, or ghosts speak to them directly or even touch them.

The cleaning staff will refuse to go on a certain floor. If booking a room, you may want to make a request to either stay where you'll get clean towels and made-up bed, or where you'll endure dirty ones in order to share a room with ghosts at no extra charge.

Bourbon Orleans Hotel
717 Orleans St.
(504) 523-2222

Prior to being turned into a luxury hotel, the Bourbon Orleans was one of New Orleans grand ballrooms where gentlemen met young Creole women to take them on as well-cared-for mistresses. In the 1800s the space went a completely different direction and became a convent for girls. Both figure into the hotel's present status as one of New Orleans' top haunted spots.

Chip Coffey, internationally acclaimed psychic and host of A&E's *Psychic Kids*, performed a reading at the historic Orleans ballroom and detected and communicated with several spirits. From the convent days, "spirited" laughter and voices are heard from the little girls that roam the halls. The most frequently told tale is of a little girl rolling her ball and chasing it down the sixth-floor corridors.

You also might want to watch your language inside the hotel. Guests have received a slap on the wrist after cursing, presumably from the ghosts of convent nuns. I guess when they prayed to be delivered into Heaven, their Lord and Master felt a four-star hotel in New Orleans came pretty damn close.

The most famous ghost at the hotel is the Lady in Red. For well over a hundred years, she's been seen frequently dancing, alone, inside the second-floor ballroom.

The Omni Royal Orleans
621 St. Louis St.
(504) 529-5333

This is a grand hotel that has received the Four Diamond luxury award for the past 31 years. Ask for a room on the second floor. If you're lucky, a maid who predates the Four Diamond awards will show up during the night to tuck you into your sheets so you don't get cold. She also likes to playfully flush the toilets or turn on the water faucets. She is, of course, a ghost.

St. Peter House
1005 Saint Peter St.
(504) 524-9232

As in most cities with an NFL franchise, there's a waiting list for Saints season tickets. Unlike Kansas City, Houston, Cincinnati, or other NFL cities, in New Orleans we also have a waiting list to check into a hotel room that was a death scene.

Johnny Thunders was the guitarist in the punk rock band the New York

Dolls. His style was described by fellow Doll Arthur Kane as "raunchy, nasty, rough, raw, and untamed. It was truly inspired." He either died or was murdered in Room 37. The room had been ransacked and most of his possessions (passport, makeup, clothes) were missing. Friends and acquaintances stated he had not been using heroin for some time, but usually did have massive doses of methadone when he traveled, none of which was found. True to their "Not Our Problem Darlin'" moniker, the NOPD did not open a criminal investigation.

If you, you know, want to stay in Room 37, you'll need to, you know, request it well ahead of time.

Myrtles Plantation
7747 US 61, St. Francisville
(225) 635-6277

Located closer to Baton Rouge than New Orleans (about 85 miles from the city), the Myrtles Plantation is worth the trip. You can take in the 120-foot veranda, exquisite ornamental ironwork, hand-painted stained glass, open-pierced frieze-work crown molding, Aubusson tapestry, Baccarat crystal chandelier, Carrara marble mantels, and gold-leafed French furnishings, and dine at the Carriage House Restaurant, where the upscale cuisine features American, Cajun, and Creole delicacies. You can also spend the night . . . if you dare. The plantation bills itself as "One of America's Most Haunted Homes."

There's a complete cast of ghosts. Chloe is a former slave who was hung on the premises for serving poisoned cake to the two little girls who lived there. The ghosts of the two murdered children have been seen playing on the veranda. William Drew Winter, an attorney who lived at Myrtles from 1860 to 1871, was shot on the side porch of the house by a stranger. Winter staggered into the house and began to climb the stairs to the second floor. He collapsed and died on the 17th step. His last dying footsteps can still be heard on the staircase to this day. The ghosts of other slaves occasionally show up to ask if they can do any chores. The grand piano has often been heard to play by itself, repeating one chord, either haunting or annoying depending on your perspective.

In addition to ghosts, Myrtles Plantation has a human-size spot on the floor that refuses to be cleaned, probably the scariest place in the state for people afflicted with contamination OCD.

Magnolia Lane Plantation, Nine Mile Point

Magnolia Lane Plantation

2141 River Rd., Nine Mile Point, LA

(504) 436-4915

As I write, you can't stay at Magnolia Lane, it's not even yet set up for official tours, but I've been talking with Richard and Brad, the father and son who live there, about the goldmine in which they live. They approved of being listed in *Fear Dat*.

Magnolia Lane is a mere 15 to 20 minutes from New Orleans (right across the Huey Long Bridge), rather than the hour and 15 minutes of Oak Alley, Laura, and other plantations. It has had a long and interesting history since the 1830s. The plantation has been used as the setting for many movies, such as *Bad Lieutenant: Port of Call New Orleans*, *Home Front*, *12 Years a Slave*, and B-movie horror films like *Venom*.

But I include it here because it's a virtual amusement park of the creepy and paranormal. TV shows *Ghost Hunters*, *Ghost Adventures*, and *Scariest Places on Earth* have all filmed segments here. There's a hanging tree where both Yankees and Rebel troops were hanged during the Civil War, depending on who controlled the property at the time. The owner, begging Northern troops not to damage his home, was shot to death and buried in a shallow grave in the front yard. On the premises is a slave graveyard. Under the house and in slave quarters are markings with voodoo scratchings that cast evil wishes on their oppressive masters.

Magnolia Lane has a bottle tree, a tree strewn with empty bottles, hung upside down to capture evil spirits and keep them away from the house. You can find bottle trees throughout the South. Cobalt blue bottles are the most desired, the brilliant color supposedly a better lure for spirits.

Best of all, in the main house, there is a room dubbed "the Dying Room." Many of Magnolia's residents died this room under mysterious circumstances. Marnie, my wife, made me promise I wouldn't enter the Dying Room during our visit. So, sitting in the hallway, I asked Richard if he'd ever had experiences with ghosts. He replied with stories of frequent noises and furniture being moved, with no greater drama than had I asked him "Have you ever watched HBO?" or "Do you ever eat cheese?"

WHERE TO EAT

Muriel's
801 Chartres St.
(504) 568-1885

Muriel's and Stanley's face each other at the intersection of Chartres and St. Ann Streets at the back corner of Jackson Square. Stanley's is haunted by tourists, while Muriel's is very much haunted by Pierre Antoine Lepardi Jourdan. Pierre built the dream home in the 1700s that since became the restaurant. Although he dearly adored his beautiful home, Jourdan could never control his gambling. In 1814 he wagered his house in a poker game and crushingly lost the one thing he treasured most. The shock was so intense, before having to vacate the premises, he committed suicide on the second floor. The staff now sets a place for him every night. Unlucky Pierre moves furniture around and occasionally hurls glasses against the wall.

Yo Mama's
727 St. Peter St.
(504) 522-1125

Yo Mama's offers video poker, televised sports, and a jukebox filled with rock and blues classics. Over 50 different tequilas line the shelves at Yo Mama's, including selections from Cuervo, Sauza, Herradura, and Patron, plus the rarest and smoothest añejos from Mexico. Oh, and one ghost.

Mr. Green previously owned a tailor shop on premise and hanged himself there. Bar employees have reported seeing a tall man with graying hair and a nice smile. He is often spotted just sitting at the bar. One bartender said he usually orders a Jack and Coke, then just disappears when you turn around. His ghost is said to have rope burns around his neck.

A bar regular reported that he has been known to tap people on the shoulder and when they turn around, no one is there. He also likes to play pool by moving the balls around on the table, and occasionally he'll pinch customers, men and women alike, on the butt. All of this makes Mr. Green sound like your most annoying friend in grade school.

Arnaud's
813 Bienville St.
(504) 523-5433

Arnaud Cazenave opened his restaurant in 1918. He was nicknamed "Count Arnaud" for his entertaining excess as he directed staff and charmed diners in the restaurant. The count's spirit is frequently felt flowing through the dining room today as it did in life. Upstairs, Arnaud's houses a Mardi Gras collection, what I've said looks and feels like Liberace's closet. Arnaud Cezanave's long-departed daughter is sometimes seen wafting through the Mardi Gras collection, complete in ball gown.

Court of Two Sisters
613 Royal St.
(504) 522-7261

The restaurant is most known for its Jazz Brunch, with over 80 items on the buffet, held out back in a gorgeous courtyard. The space was once occupied by the Camor sisters, Emma and Bertha. They had a shop selling perfumes and gowns from Paris. The sisters were inseparable in life and died very closely one after the other. Restaurant staff and diners have discovered they are equally inseparable on the other side. They are often seen sitting or strolling, arm in arm, in their beloved courtyard.

The Bombay Club

830 Conti St.

(504) 586-0972

The Bombay Club has a low-lit, warm, one might say "clubby" feel. The award-winning restaurant serves over 115 different kinds of martinis. It also has one additional spirit, that of a deceased madam from nearby Storyville, a former red-light district. She was and is attracted to the sophisticated set and enjoys the finer things in life. Her curvaceous but deceased figure is often seen sashaying through the dining area and around the romantically situated booths. But be careful. They say once you go ghost, all other sex is toast. Ask Kesha.

WHERE TO DRINK

Lafitte Blacksmith Shop

941 Bourbon St.

Supposedly owned by Jean Lafitte (though there's no record of that fact), this is said to be where he operated a blacksmith shop as a seemingly legitimate business to serve as a front for his pirating enterprises. The bar is where Lafitte headquartered his smuggling operation and where he hid much of his stolen gold. The Lafitte Blacksmith is also the oldest bar in the United States, dating back to the 1720s. It still has no electricity, except for the ATM and gaming machines. The bar has the distinction of being one of the few remaining original French-built structures in New Orleans after the great fire of 1788 and the pretty okay fire of 1794 destroyed the vast majority.

You can differentiate the French buildings from the largely Spanish ones in the Quarter by the steeply pitched roofs. When the displaced Acadians arrived from Canada, they continued to build in the same style used up north, with roofs designed to keep snow from piling up and adding weight. Since snow accumulates about once every 30 years in New Orleans, the style of the Lafitte bar and other French buildings is not exactly needed here.

In the center, or evil heart, of the bar is a fireplace. The fireplace is surrounded by what some describe as "an unwholesome aura," complete with cold spots. Staff and patrons claim to have seen a pair of watchful red eyes'

Ghost Hunter Kevin Betzer

It's easier to dismiss ghosts in the daylight.
    —Patricia Briggs, fantasy author best known for the Mercy Thompson series

Ghosts have been around for all of recorded history and a part of every culture across the planet. Calling on the spirits of the dead for guidance or protection goes back at least to Confucianism (around 500 BC).

Interaction with ghosts hit a pop culture zenith in the mid to late 1800s, when séances were as popular as Instagram and Nicki Minaj are now. Getting a seat at the table with celebrity-level mediums like Cora Lodencia Veronica Scott, America's top audile, was then as desired and as difficult to score as Super Bowl tickets.

Everyone attended séances back then, even Abraham Lincoln did so *inside the White House*, though he might have been dragged to the table by his spirit-seeking wife, Mary Todd, the same way husbands today are dragged to any movie starring Hugh Grant. And it wasn't just honest Abe. FDR attended séances. Nancy Reagan was known for having woo-woo thoughts inside that enormous head of hers.

Ghosts, like everything, are subject to and the victim of fashion. As Motown has given way to hip-hop and rap, so, too, séances have become sweetly nostalgic, replaced by high-tech ghost hunting. Ghost hunting has a fairly long history itself. The Ghost Club formed in London in 1862, boasting such members as famous novelists Charles Dickens and Sir Arthur Conan Doyle, poet William Butler Yeats, and actor in practically every horror movie produced by Hammer, Peter Cushing. The purpose of the Ghost Club was to investigate alleged hauntings.

In the 1960s and '70s, the Great White Hunters of ghosts were Hans Holzer in the United States and Peter Underwood in England. Both were best-selling authors of many books about the paranormal. Hans Holzer is most famous for his investigation of the "Amityville Horror" house. Peter Underwood has been called the "King of Ghost Hunters." His *50* books offer step-by-step practical advice for the paranormal investigator and remain the definitive standard-bearer on the topic. His books are a ghost hunter's version of evergreen best sellers like *The Joy of Cooking*.

Ghost hunters themselves have, in recent years, undergone a complete makeover.

I credit Doctors Spengler, Venkman, and Stantz as being the primary cause for the revolution. Ghost hunting has gone high-tech. A contemporary ghost hunter isn't

Kevin Betzer

taken seriously unless armed with an electromagnetic field meter (EMF), laser thermometers, and closed-circuit surveillance systems.

The Travel Channel and the SyFy Channel have gotten rich off reality TV shows like *Ghost Hunters* and *America's Scariest and Most Haunted Places*. Jason Hawes, *Ghost Hunters'* star, is a plumber by trade but ghost hunter by passion.

Most recently, ghost hunting groups like the Paranormal Hot Squad, a team of models and underemployed actresses, offer you to opportunity to "film sexy sleepovers in the scariest, most haunted locations," and Paranormal Xpeditions, which bills itself as having three of the hottest female investigators who will "scare you stiff," seek to fulfill dual desires for hauntings and honeys.

New Orleans' rising star hunter is Kevin Betzer. Looking more like he belongs onstage with Cypress Hill or Calle 13 rather than one of the old Ghost Club members, Kevin's become the face of *Deep South Paranormal* on the SyFy Channel along with TV partner Chris Melancon, founder of NOLA Ghost Hunting Tours.

Hurricane Katrina had a serendipitous hand in all this. Kevin grew up in Chalmette, just outside New Orleans. Katrina completely wiped out his childhood home. The family moved to Kenner, right next door to Randy Hardy. The neighboring boys became instant best friends. Although Randy was the more skeptical, both boys were into the paranormal. They began doing amateur hour experiments after school and on weekends.

Inside Lafayette Cemetery #1, the two came across an open tomb with nothing inside. They decided, in a way only teens would choose, "Why not crawl in a cemetery vault and do an EVP session?" While inside the tomb, the two asked questions with a recorder going. They heard nothing at the time. The next day, when they replayed the tape, there was a whispered but clear voice telling them, "Leave! Leave now!"

The two were hooked.

Kevin couldn't wait for free time to check old plantations, seedy locations in the French Quarter, and haunted homes for more evidence.

Kevin and Randy started making videos of their investigations and posting them on YouTube. While they took the investigations seriously, the fun they were having was also very self-evident. A few weeks after their first YouTube video, Kevin received a call from a TV producer asking if they'd be interested in doing a show. They replied, "HELL, YEAH!" faster than they'd jumped into their first open tomb. Randy took on the role as the daredevil of *Deep South Paranormal*. Kevin was the guy with all the tools and gadgets.

After filming the first season, Kevin wanted to open up a business to help educate others in paranormal investigations. He hooked up with Chris Melancon, founder of the Paranormal Society of New Orleans, and created NOLA Ghost Hunting Tours.

As the gadget guy, Kevin can talk for hours about the advances in ghost-hunting equipment and the latest hot app. When I asked him for the hottest or most essential tool in ghost hunting, he waxed poetically about the recently introduced Echovox System 2.5. Echovox is a mobile monetization company focused on monetizing web and traditional media audiences with transaction-enabled mobile services. In English, that means the machine creates a sort of white noise that spirits are able to use to enable them to form words and communicate with the living. Best of all, Echovox is an app you can download on your phone. So, now your phone can keep your schedule, take selfies, and talk to the dead.

But whether you use Echovox, the K2 EMF Meter with mini-downsizing rods, or the old-fashioned "I believe in Mary Worth, I believe in Mary Worth," the key thing will always be the ghosts themselves.

I asked Kevin what was the spookiest experience he's encountered. He responded, "My strangest experiences are when I see someone physically get scratched. I've seen it a couple of times. I always ask myself, how is that even possible? But it happens. It's very creepy!"

Being scratched by a ghost has happened several times at the Jimani Lounge (141 Chartres Street). This was a gay bar in The French Quarter where on June 24, 1973, 32 people died as a result of an intentionally set fire. The most likely suspect, a man who had been thrown out of the bar earlier in the day, was never charged.

NOLA Ghost Tours regularly bump into five identifiable ghosts inside the Jimani Lounge. While getting scratched is rare, tour takers have often been touched by a ghost and have had their names called out.

"When you walk inside Jimani, you can just feel the energy," said Kevin. "Something is there for sure."

studying them through the fireplace grate. If you sit at a table near the fireplace, you may join the number of people who have reported being touched by a cold, ghostly hand.

The entity of Jean Lafitte himself has been seen in the upstairs ladies' restroom. Women have entered an empty stall and reported hearing footsteps and the sound of sighs in nearby stalls. One woman reported hearing a sudden peal of laughter from the stall areas when only she was inside. I guess Jean likes the ladies in death as much as he did in life.

The Bourbon Pub
801 Bourbon St.

Downstairs, the Bourbon Pub is a saloon. Upstairs is a dance club with a balcony overlooking Bourbon Street. The club blasts what New Orleans would consider "alternative" music. Jazz, blues, and bounce are replaced by disco and techno music. It is a wildly popular hangout with the gay community.

While straights are welcomed, they'll be greatly outnumbered. Someone presumed to be a straight woman is a frequent and more than welcome guest, called "Mam" by the bar's staff.

Mam is the ghost of a diminutive Creole slave lady, who often appears walking through the mostly empty bar area in the early morning hours. She wears an old cotton dress, her head is covered in a bandana, and she carries a large wooden spoon. Walking and muttering to herself, she sometimes stops and looks directly at staff members before she disappears into the shadows. Cups often move across the bar on their own. Footsteps are heard walking across the empty second floor's haunted balcony.

These acts may be Mam's, or they could be the Bastinado Ghost's. Anytime of the day or night, unsuspecting patrons have been resting comfortably at the bar when, out of nowhere, they are hit on the foot by what they describe as feeling like being struck with a hard stick. Some have likened it to an in-the-know form of S&M known as Bastinado, where the soles of the feet are struck with a wooden pole as a form of sexual arousal. This weird phalangeal assault has happened so often at the Bourbon Pub that the spirit has been nicknamed "the Bastinado Ghost," and some regulars are disappointed to have never been struck by him.

Cafe Lafitte in Exile

901 Bourbon St.

Lafitte in Exile is the oldest gay bar in the country. It was created when the owner of Lafitte Blacksmith Shop went out of his way to make his increasingly gay clientele uncomfortable and clearly unwelcome. So, regular patron Tom Caplinger opened a gay friendly bar a half-block away.

During their years in New Orleans, Tennessee Williams and Truman Capote used to frequent Lafitte in Exile. Tennessee's ghost is said to turn up quite often sitting at the end of the bar, sipping a cocktail. Truman's ghost haunts the small stairwell leading to the second floor and very often has been captured on video and film. Some say he even strikes up little stair-side chats.

A ghost named Mr. Bubby trumps the two great writers. Mr. Bubby is said to be a frisky and fun-loving spirit who cuts it up on the dance floor, waves to Bourbon Street tourists from the balcony, and has been known to pinch a butt or two.

Old Absinthe House

240 Bourbon St.

Built in 1807, this location originally held a local importing firm, then converted to a neighborhood grocery that imported fine foods, tobaccos, and wines from all over the world. As a bar, it became nationally famous when owned by Owen Brennan. The gregarious patriarch to the many Brennan owner restaurants, Owen had an infectious mix of hospitality and showmanship that made the bar a regular stop for visiting celebrities like Frank Sinatra, Clark Gable, and Liza Minnelli. Earlier it had been Teddy Roosevelt's must-go place in New Orleans and was been patronized by Oscar Wilde, P. T. Barnum, Mark Twain, Jenny Lind, Enrico Caruso, and General Robert E Lee.

Maybe it was to hang out with celebrities or vice versa, but the bar has also been frequented by an A-list of ghosts: Jean Lafitte, Andrew Jackson, Benjamin "The Beast" Butler, and Marie Laveau herself.

Less famous apparitions show up on an almost daily basis. They move bottles and glasses behind the bar, rock chairs back and forth, and open and close the bar doors.

Local legend has it that the Old Absinthe House sits atop a series of old tunnels, dug by Jean Lafitte and his pirates, to link him to stored goods and provide a quick getaway, if needed. As with many "facts" about Jean Lafitte, there is no evidence of such tunnels.

Alibi Bar
811 Iberville St.

Two doors up from Bourbon Street, the Alibi is popular as a late-night hangout. *Playboy* and *Stuff* magazines have featured the Alibi among the best bars in New Orleans. Past midnight, it will mostly be stuffed with people working in the many New Orleans service jobs. They share space with Davie, the ghost of another service worker, an ex-employee of the bar, who still wants to wait on customers.

There's a less helpful ghost known for hurling glasses, bottles, and cutlery from the bar onto the floor and occasionally in the direction of staff members. This ghost is supposedly a man stabbed to death behind the bar.

Only employees are permitted to go into the attic, not that they want to, either. This area is said to be the most haunted. Legend has it that the attic was once a makeshift hiding place for escaped slaves waiting for passage on the Underground Railroad. The sounds of sighs and soft crying have often been heard near the old attic door.

After visiting New Orleans and staying in haunted hotels, eating in haunted restaurants, and getting sloppy in haunted bars, you may choose to move here, as I did. Did you know that home sellers are required to disclose if their property is haunted, or as the law reads, "psychologically impacted"? There was an actual case, but in Nyack, New York, not New Orleans, where a buyer, Jeffrey Stambovsky, got his money back from the seller, Helen Ackley. The New York Supreme Court justices were "moved by the spirit of equity" to rule that they make no claim as to whether poltergeists actually exist, but, based on wide reports of the house's haunted status, that it was haunted as a matter of law.

Genius
Palmistry
&
TAROT
Counseling
Since 1967
Member of
mensa

Seasoned psychic in Jackson Square KATHLEEN PARKER

CHAPTER 7

Rare Mediums

There's a spirit to this city. This city has a soul. If you can sense it, you don't want to go anywhere else.
—**Maria Shaw Lawson, psychic contributor to** *National Enquirer* **and**
Soap Opera Digest **and ex-pat-yat, transplanted from Detroit to New Orleans**

I first realized I was psychic next Monday. —**Dean Cavanagh**

Most cities wake up with the sound of garbage trucks' compressing trash and the sight of produce trucks' delivering their goods to not-yet-open restaurants. In New Orleans, mornings are met with street psychics' popping out their tables and chairs and staking out territory on Jackson Square.

Some have called them cosmic carpetbaggers, street urchins whom have come from elsewhere to take advantage of New Orleans' psychic vibe and rip off tourists with their mumbo-jumbo. I sat down with a New Orleans street psychic once. I "felt" she had more legitimacy than the gaggle of other street psychics lining the square. I learned my "feelings" were about as reliable as Fox News. She predicted I was about to come into great wealth. This happened to be right before my financial world went into free fall. Maybe I met this particular psychic on Opposite Day.

Psychics, mediums, and tarot card readers have been around "forever." Well, kinda-sorta forever, as shamans and medicine men date back to early tribes in prerecorded history. In ancient Egypt, the priests of Ra at Memphis acted as seers. Assyrian prophets were called *nabu*, or "to call" or "announce." The Bible has several references to prophets like Samuel and Daniel. And, of course, there is the famous Oracle at Delphi, whose prophecies guided Apollo.

The earliest form of fortune-telling was astrology, whereby practitioners used relative positions of planets and stars to gain insight into people's lives and predict their futures. True story: When I joined a major book publisher as its sales director, I struck up an immediate friendship with two marketing directors. They paid for a noted astrologer to "do" me when she visited from California. The astrologer told me I was not happy at my job (which I was not), that the place felt like a funnel of papers swirling out of control (which it did), and that I was thinking of leaving the company for a better job (which I was). She then said, "Don't go. You were meant to run this place." Six months later I was offered and accepted the job as head of the company.

It's not hard to dismiss or ridicule many psychics. Research by the James Randi Educational Foundation and StopSylvia.com revealed famous psychic detective Sylvia Browne was basically a hack clairvoyant. She claimed to solve murders and missing person cases in her weekly predictions on *The Montel Williams Show*. She got it wrong in 115 of her 115 predictions. 115 out of 115! You could pull random slips of paper out of a borrowed hat and do better than she did. Sylvia Browne wasn't just bad making psychic predictions, she was preternaturally bad.

Theresa Caputo, dubbed the "Long Island Medium" in the current reality TV show of the same name, has been characterized as a cross between Samantha from *Bewitched* and one of the Real Housewives of New Jersey. Of late, she has been attacked more and more, and not just for her helmet hair. A private detective was brought in to unmask Caputo as a fake. He did uncover some creative editing of her TV show, which eliminated all of her many wrong readings and predictions. More damningly, he discovered pre-interviews were being conducted with the people with whom Theresa would later "randomly" or "accidentally" bump into while taping the show. Her "spontaneous psychic messages" were clearly not gleaned by her gifts, but from the earlier interviews.

However, as one source put it, "Caputo may be a fake, we find her personally very likable and we find her show to be highly entertaining and enjoyable."

In 1988 the US National Academy of Sciences issued a report that concluded there is "no scientific justification from research conducted over a period of 130 years for the existence of parapsychological phenomena." But then, the NAS is situated on Constitution Avenue, midway between the Department of State and the Daughters of the Revolution Constitution Hall.

If you want legitimate statements of fact, I think Washington, DC, is the last place I'd turn.

Here in New Orleans, we do have legitimate and informed tour guides, but also babbling make-it-up-as-they-go hucksters. There are places you can buy "real" (not-to-be-played-with) voodoo amulets and gris-gris bags, but far more numerous spots to get made-in-China voodoo dolls. So, too, we have the easily debunked psychic readers and the bona fide.

I don't want to issue a blanket statement that all the horde of street psychics on Jackson Square should be considered members of the huckster class. Among the cheap T-shirts and sunglasses in the French Market, you can sometimes find a rare treasure. All NFL players didn't come from football factories like Alabama or Florida State. Kurt Warner bagged groceries before becoming the Super Bowl MVP. So, too, in the sea of four-flushers lining Jackson Square, there are a few legitimate psychics.

Zaar has split his time doing readings on Jackson Square and in Voodoo Authentica for over 15 years. He has appeared reading tarot on Bridezilla and palms on Girls Next Door.

Willow Le Mechant has been a longtime Jackson Square–sitting soothsayer. She's been doing readings professionally for over 20 years but has been communicating with the other side since she was in diapers. Her mother pulled her aside to explain her gifts when she was 13. The young Willow had foreseen her father's death, though he was only 43 years old.

Over the years, Willow has built up a loyal clientele: some locals who see her once a month and visitors from other cities who drop in for their annual or half-yearly psychic checkup. She's ever expanding her business. Willow became ordained as a minister in 1999 and is now able to legally oversee unique, themed weddings and handfastings, specializing in Wiccan, Gothic, vampire, steampunk ceremonies, same-sex unions, and most anything else. At the time of my writing, she is preparing to take her talents off the square and open the Divine Source Spiritual Center, a longtime dream dedicated to the memory of her father. Until his too-young death in 1975, he'd been very politically active and a lifetime humanitarian, fighting for civil rights in the '60s; a union president for the UAW for 23 years; and a 4-H leader. Her goal is to serve others, using her and others' psychic gifts.

The Divine Source, on Rampart Street along the edge of the French Quarter, will be a place of healing the mind, body, and spirit through Reiki/ Rising Star, spiritual guidance, tarot/palm reading/mediumship, art, music, astrology, past life regression, hypnotherapy, yoga, meditation, and healing circles. The building will be three stories. The first floor will be a metaphysical shop with readings and healings. The second story will be an event hall with a stage and a very old and beautiful grand piano, available for weddings, parties, and other events. The third floor will be living quarters for practicing spiritualists and for visitors desiring something more spiritual than the Embassy Suites.

Cari Roy, profiled in greater length in this chapter, has been called the #1 psychic in America. She has said of New Orleans, "I have long called it a 'petri dish of the paranormal' and a 'paranormal amusement park.' There is always some otherworldly dimension that is operating here and you only need to know where to go and how to connect for you to have a paranormal experience. The entire city is haunted, every brick has been bled on." But she also told me during my visit, "Sometimes the eerie sigh heard in the next room is just faulty plumbing."

Detroit native and psychic Maria Shaw Lawson had made numerous trips to New Orleans over the years. She and her husband, Joe, a paranormal investigator, used to travel to hot spots for both their careers. They purchased a French Quarter home in 2000 and finally moved here in 2011, Maria stating, "There's a spirit to this city. This city has a soul. If you can sense it, you don't want to go anywhere else."

Before her psychic career, Lawson worked at a daily paper and on the evening news in Michigan. Her biological mother (she is adopted) encouraged her to study astrology, which she compared to learning a foreign language. Years later, her astrological column now appears every week in the *National Enquirer* and regularly in *Soap Opera Digest*. Maria created the New Orleans Psychic Fair at the House of Broel in the Garden District (2220 St. Charles Avenue). Each January, Maria Shaw Lawson and other psychics conduct lectures, classes and readings. The fair also offers a special "crossing over" session in which she will contact the other side.

The most long-standing and noteworthy spot for readings is Bottom of the Cup (327 Chartres Street). Readings have been held there since 1929, displaying the foresight to open a business right at start of the Great Depression. But it did survive and now stands as a psychic version of venerable New Orleans destinations like Commander's Palace restaurant or Preservation Hall music venue.

It started out as a tearoom, where shoppers could relax in the middle

Maria Shaw Lawson   <small>ARTHUR SEVERIO</small>

or at the end of hitting every retailer in the French Quarter. After a patron drank a cup of tea, a psychic would come by the table and read the leaves. The Bottom of the Cup still serves tea—it carries over one hundred brands— but is now best known for its metaphysical gifts, hanging charms, crystal balls, tarot card decks, and, above all else, its psychic readers. The Cup also provides an audio recording of your session, so you can go back to refresh mantas you were supposed to repeat or you can check the veracity of predictions made.

Adele Mullen, who passed away in 2007 and is buried in the Metairie Cemetery, was one of the more famous readers. She left her career as a teacher to join the family business and discovered her gifts for predicting the future exceeded her talents for correcting grammar or teaching multiplication tables. During her ownership of Bottom of the Cup, national TV and radio networks sought her out for annual Super Bowl predictions.

Had she lived another two years, I'm sure she would have foreseen Sean Peyton's onside kick to start the second half. She consulted with law enforcement agencies throughout the country on suspect profiling, though she

PROFILE:
Cari Roy

Cari Roy has been rated the #1 psychic in America. She's sort of our Emeril Lagasse or Fats Domino of clairvoyants. To visit her, you enter the Exchange Centre, an innocuous 21-story, 84,000-square-foot office building in the Central Business District. You check in with the uniformed security guards seated in monochrome blandness behind a tan counter, surrounded by taupe-colored walls, and then cross a broad expanse of highly polished floor to take the elevator to her office. There, you're led to a room in which there are no talismans, no skulls, no incense. About the only unusual detail is a Buddha fountain with a multicolored spinning ball. Cari herself was an unassuming petite blonde in a sleeveless midnight blue summer dress. The entire experience felt about as mystical as visiting a financial planner or marriage counselor.

And that is exactly as she intends. Cari insists there's nothing unusual about her gifts. Everyone has them. She's just better plugged into the psychic realm, the way other people run faster or are better at math. Her readings are not intended as shock-and-awe experiences, but rather to provide psychic and medium information to give clarity, positive direction, and peace of mind. Her clients have referred to their readings as "a massage for the soul" and "better than a valium." She remarked that she considers it an honor that so many trust her in their time of need. "I care deeply for the well-being of my clients and they can sense that."

Cari was always inclined or predisposed toward psychic work, as her grandfather had been a numerologist and astrologist and her mother was a psychic medium. As a child, she participated in séances in parlors with drapes drawn tight. She would also, on occasion, pass by a room to spy her mother talking to an empty chair. The chair was sometimes rocking back and forth.

Cari lived many places as the well-traveled daughter of a renowned operatic bass: New York, Paris, and New Orleans. As she notes, "Growing up, I spent a lot of my time in New Orleans. I was always awestruck by the intense level of spiritual energy combined with the mysterious sense of timelessness of this city. I'd have visions of having lived here in the past and living here again in the future and I made a vow to settle back here when I completed my formal education." She did so in 1990. Like me, she is never leaving.

Cari Roy's first hints that she had psychic gifts happened when she was seven years old. She would catch glimpses of apparitions or spirits at the base of her bed. The same year, a man approached her when she and her mother were shopping at a department store. This was an era, now gone, when parents felt safe leaving their children alone as they browsed a different department. The man came up to Cari and asked if she wanted

Cari Roy

to see his watch. When she later described the man and his watch in detail, her mother knew exactly who had approached the young girl: A relative for whom his watch was his prized possession. A relative who had died years earlier.

Once confirmed she had psychic gifts, Cari said the most important thing her mother taught her is how to turn it off. Not only would it be exhausting to receive a constant flow of messages and images from "the other side" but, in controlling her gift, she can also turn it on and be more intensely present and focused when doing actual readings.

Cari does pure psychic readings, meaning she doesn't use tarot cards, palmistry, or crystal balls. It's not that she discredits these as props, but she does feel they give the reader an "out" or the ability to not take full responsibility for their reading, as if the cards have a mind of their own. She feels that "ultimately the psychic buck stops with me and the accuracy or not of the reading is mine."

She's been featured in several documentaries filmed in New Orleans, appeared in A&E's *Haunted Houses: Tortured Souls and Restless Spirits*, The Travel Channel's *America's Most Terrifying Places*, ISPR's *New Orleans—Rich and Haunted*, and on the *Today Show*. TravelChannel.com named her "New Orleans most renowned psychic and New Orleans' best psychic to see." This was prior to BBC America's naming her the #1 psychic in America. She is also a regularly featured guest on local New Orleans news stations and radio shows.

Cari's business is now thriving with a mix of first-timers and regulars. Some come for their annual reading just as they'd visit their doctor once a year for a physical or drop off their car for oil change, lube, and tire rotation. While many customers are New Orleans based, an equal number are visitors wanting to take in the unique New Orleans vibe when they visit this psychic hallowed ground. Over time, a significant number of out-of-towners have become regulars. After receiving one call from Utica, New York, she's become *the* psychic of Utica, with numerous regulars calling down to New Orleans after that lone first customer spread the word of mouth throughout the "Second Chance City" or "The City That God Forgot" (two of Utica's monikers).

Her customer base is also a wildly divergent mix, from investment bankers trying to supplement their market research to one-time gangbangers wanting her to contact a murdered fellow gang member to identify his shooter. That one frankly scared the beje-sus out of her.

As for so many in New Orleans, Hurricane Katrina had a huge impact. Cari foresaw the devastation of Katrina and that it would be by water, not wind. While the storm was just starting to swirl in the Gulf, Cari said the spirit of her departed mother showed her what was to come. She closed her eyes and saw her mother swimming to her underwa-ter. After that, she said, "I warned anyone I could, gave out some pet carriers, and got myself out of Dodge." She also saw that it would take nearly five years to come back and predicted on local radio that the Saints would win the Super Bowl to mark the year of New Orleans' renewal.

At first, with so much destroyed or shuttered, Cari joined a small stream of locals who would cluster at BJ's Lounge in Bywater, one of the few bars that reopened. BJ's is a classic juke joint. The cash-only bar has a bartender who's worked there for over 20 years; most of the patrons know each other, and King James and the Special Men blast their sweaty vintage R&B every Monday night. After the storm, Cari said, "It was where we met up, drank, ate our government-issued MREs. Huddled in a bar was a very New Orleans way to have group therapy for our collective PTSD. We didn't have heat or hot water but we had each other and our Katrina stories."

As a top psychic, Cari is consistently spot-on in her readings and predictions, but she does not claim infallibility. She recommends that if a psychic claims 100 percent accuracy, run like hell. Even New Orleans' best chefs like Susan Spicer and Paul Prud-homme have off nights. Drew Brees does, on rare occasion, throw three interceptions in a game.

During our visit, in which she generously gave me nearly three hours, we talked about most everything, including politics, social media, and documentary films. However, if you're a client paying by the hour, I suggest you stick with your career and love inter-ests, dead relatives, or what will get you out of the current mess of your life.

Cari did mix in personal readings, but I doubt the specifics of *my* reading make good material for *your* reading. I'll just note that, not surprisingly, she was quite accurate about my past and hopefully unerring about my future.

Cari did say that my traveler's trilogy of books would lead to something bigger, pos-sibly involving TV or film. A month later, out of the blue, I was contacted about hosting a new show on the Travel Channel. I doubt I'll get the part, but you never know. Maybe by the time you read this I will also be on your TV screen as an older, plumper version of Guy Fieri, but hopefully less annoying. Cari also said that after reading *Fear Dat*, you would buy multiple copies for friends, relatives, and perfect strangers who look like they needed a pick-me-up. (Kidding.)

Our session ended with a hug at the elevator. As Cari noted, "All my sessions end with a hug, whether they want one or not."

Bottom of the Cup   DEB DELLA PIANA

always found this work distressing. Adele's clients included people from all walks of life, including oil executives, politicians, and entertainers.

Today's star is Otis Briggs. He's been doing readings at the Cup since 1972 and definitely has "the look" of a seer, something like the love child of Truman Capote and Georgia O'Keeffe. Otis is a versatile psychic, reading tea leaves, tarot cards, or the ridges and lines of your palm, or doing straight-up pure psychic readings using only his naturally ability. He has been featured in numerous print and media specials, with topics ranging from his serious forecast of the economy to Otis's appearing as a reader on the TLC's *Little Couple.*

Of course, like any psychic, master chef or financial adviser, he is not 100 percent infallible. When the BCS football championship was played in New Orleans in 2012, Otis predicted, "Things will work out good for LSU." He said. "LSU will score at least twenty points. LSU is going to run over them [Alabama]. They've really got it together." His prediction was no better than his grammar. The Crimson Tide won 21–0.

Maybe Richard Jefferson, LSU's quarterback who had a miserable championship game, was paid off by Yesteryear's, a competing psychic store in the Quarter, to make Otis look bad. Yesteryear's (626 Bourbon Street) sells masks, books, and handmade dolls in addition to offering tarot or palm readings by the resident psychics. Kala Jackson, a reader at Yesteryear's, has, like Adele Mullen, consulted with the police on some cases.

Golden Leaves is a third noted establishment, a bookstore and center for metaphysical studies (and, of course, readings). It is located just outside the city, near the Lakeside Mall, at 211 Phlox Street in Metairie. The store provides resources and supplies for professional and amateur psychics, mediums, astrologers, clairvoyants, shamans, and healers. It's pretty much the Michael's or Dick's Sporting Goods for anyone into woo-woo. Golden Leaves holds a Metaphysical Fair every third Friday of the month.

Also in Metairie is the Metaphysical Resource Center (1708 Lake Avenue). If Golden Leaves is a woo-woo Michael's or Dick's, the resource center would have to be the Walmart or Costco of woo-woo. After Hurricane Katrina destroyed a large number of locations for independent psychics and healers, the center brought many under one roof for services and education, the center boasts a huge network of a staff skilled in astrology, card reading, as mediums, massage therapy, spiritual counseling, Reiki healing, grief counseling, polarity therapy, past life regression therapy, a law of attraction coach, a Keytonic Science scholar, a shamanic practitioner, and a remote viewer psychodynamatist. I have no idea of the meaning of half the things I just listed.

If you are specifically into astrology, Lynn Wilson was New Orleans' premier astrologer. For 20 years, she ran her business from her apartment in the Warehouse District. She correctly predicted the flooding of the city in 2005. She nailed former mayor Ray Nagin in 2008, noting he had the very rare "grand square." Lynn explained his unusual alignment of planetary influences: "It is literally a square, with four planets (Mercury, Mars, Pluto, and Saturn) at 90-degree angles to one another." She said, "People with grand squares tend to live more stress-filled lives." Ray's next 10 years will also be jail cell filled, in federal prison.

Sadly, the only way you can partake of Lynn's services now is to use an afterlife channeler, and I'm not so sure using an afterlife channeler to get insights from a no-longer-alive astrologer might not result in some sort of *Being John Malkovich*–type disaster.

Though you can't visit her, I've included her here because of some poignant statements she made about post-Katrina New Orleans. Lynn predicted on her website that our city will remain unlike the rest of urban America. "I don't see it ever being a clean, efficient, crime-free city," she said. "And I think people who live there need to love it for what it is—a celebration of the senses and a place where you can immerse yourself in the creative juices caused by this flow, which can serve as a form of compost for creativity and soul work. New Orleans value to the world lies in its charming dysfunctionality. The world doesn't need more Atlantas. We need a place where 'slow' is accepted as the treasure that it is."

A typical night in New Orleans

Louis Maistros

CHAPTER 8

Celebrations *in the* Big Queasy

We dance even if there's no radio. We drink at funerals. We talk too much and laugh too loud and live too large and, frankly, we're suspicious of others who don't.
—**Chris Rose, columnist, commentator, and author of** *1 Dead in Attic*

Everyone in this good city enjoys the full right to pursue his own inclinations in all reasonable and, unreasonable ways.
—*The Daily Picayune,* **New Orleans, March 5, 1851**

New Orleans will celebrate pretty much anything. We have festivals for gumbo, po'boys, Creole tomatoes, White Linen Night (people wear white linen and stroll the art galleries on Julia Street while drinking white wine and listening to live music), Dirty Linen Night (people wear whatever they want, drink whatever they want, and stroll the art galleries in the Quarter), the Red Dress Run (a mini-marathon sponsored by the New Orleans Hash House Harriers, a self-proclaimed "drinking club with a running problem," in which men and women dress in red dresses for running . . . and drinking), and my personal favorite, San Fermin in Nueva Orleans (a running of the bulls in which the bulls are members of the Big Easy Roller Girls on skates, wearing helmets with horns, and armed with plastic baseball bats to whack the butts of any unfortunate white-clad runner they catch).

My first Easter living in the city, my daughter asked what time was the parade. I replied, "Do you mean the Historic French Quarter Easter Parade which begins at nine forty-five A.M. in front of Antoine's, or the one P.M. Chris Owens French Quarter Easter Parade, or the four P.M. Official Gay Easter Parade?"

Anytime you visit New Orleans, there will most likely be a festival (or two) or parade (or three) celebrating "something." Somebody paid an electric bill and got the lights turned back on? It's party time!

You may want to plan a visit here around a particularly creepy event. None are any creepier than the Decadence Festival each August, but that'd be for other reasons, like the large number of overweight and overly hairy men running around the French Quarter, wearing nothing but leather chaps with their naked, dimpled butts hanging out for all the world to avert its eyes.

New Orleans' own Running of the Bulls—in skates   <small>KATHLEEN PARKER</small>

Halloween is probably more to most people's liking. Not shockingly, we do know how to "do" Halloween.

Like New York's West Village, we have a first-rate Halloween parade. Unlike New York, we have *two* first-rate parades. The Jim Monaghan parade is celebrating its 18th year. The parade starts at Molly's Market in the French Market and ends with a costume contest at Erin Rose Bar on Conti. There's also the Krewe du Boo Parade, with floats produced by Blaine Kern, and bands and groups like the Krewe of Rolling Elvi (Elvis impersonators on motorized bikes) or the Bearded Oysters (kind of self-explanatory), but mostly everyday people in costume.

Add at least an hour to the posted starting time of both. The Halloween parades tend to be as punctual as Mardi Gras parades or streetcars or bands playing at Tipitina's or pretty much everything else in New Orleans (i.e., not at all).

Like every city, town, and suburb, we have haunted house attractions.

The elaborate House of Shock, right outside New Orleans in Jefferson (319 Butterworth Street), is rated the #1 haunted house in the country by people who rate such things. Annually, more than 25,000 people will pay $25 to encounter Phil Anselmo's legendary attraction that offers live actors portraying freaks and ghouls amid faux graveyards, butcher shops, swamps, and a cultish church. National acts and pyrotechnics kick it up a notch from the average pumpkin patch or corn maze. The attraction opens September 30 and runs every Friday and Saturday through early November.

I'll make a little altar, maybe with sacrifices, to ensure that House of Shock remains open for your visit. At the time I write this book, there is a rumor it will close after 21 years.

Every bit as popular with locals is the Mausoleum, because it's located in the city proper (3400 Canal Street), easily accessed straight up the Canal Street streetcar line appropriately named "Cemeteries." The massive mansion is the former P.J. McHahon Funeral Home. Inside, the made-up monster staff do things I thought were illegal. I'd always heard employees were not allowed to touch you in haunted house attractions. Here, they find ways to distract you and physically separate you from your group. What's scarier than suddenly realizing you are . . . all . . . alone? In the night. In the dark. All alone.

Just outside New Orleans proper are additional haunted houses: The Chamber of Horrors, the Colonial Shopping Center, 7335 Jefferson Highway in Harahan; Bernie Baxter's Traveling Sideshow, 44 Vivian Court, Algiers; and the farther, but worth the trip, 13th Gate and Necropolis 13, 832 St. Philip Street, in Baton Rouge.

In addition to haunted houses, New Orleans has haunted boat attractions. The Creole Queen has live music, an open bar, costume contest, and silent auction where donations are made to provide services for the homeless. The Jean Lafitte Swamp & Airboat Tours hosts Boat Rides of Terror, a haunted swamp tour where gators, snakes, and the cornball jokes of your tour guide become even more horrifying and are amplified with live music on the shore. Tours run continuously from 7:15 P.M. till 11:00 P.M.

The Audubon Zoo stays open past its normal hours for Boo at the Zoo, nights of entertainment, food, trick-or-treating, and kid-appropriate, not-so-scary stories. The Audubon Insectarium (423 Canal Street) offers the Crawloween, which includes bug crafts, trick-or-treating, and lectures about misunderstood arthropods: spiders, roaches, and maggots. The Windsor Court Hotel hosts a Creepy Crawly Children's Tea. City Park holds Ghost in the Oaks (usually a week before Halloween) from 6:00 P.M. to 10 P.M. in the Carousel Gardens Amusement Park and includes food and music.

The French Quarter each year puts on the Boo Carré Halloween & Harvest Festival, with miniature golf, a photo booth, Halloween crafts, a costume contest, and pumpkin painting. The Cabildo sponsors the Ghostly Gallivant fund-raiser and walking tour. The Hotel Monteleone hosts an annual ball to honor its many ghosts. Dirty Coast, proprietors of exceptionally designed local T-shirts, hosts a Halloween costume party at Studio 3 (3610 Tchoupitoulas Street) with live music, DJs, and a costume contest. The Museum of Art shows nighttime outdoor screenings of scary movies. Last year it showed *Rosemary's Baby*, which, with its devil rape scene, might have caused a church lady uproar in other cities. Here, not so much.

For your dog, there's the Howl-o-Ween Pawtay at the Times Grill (1896 N. Causeway), a dog-friendly benefit for the Humane Society, with live music and a dog costume contest.

The kiddies and pets would not be welcomed at the Allways Lounge's Halloween Fun House (2240 St. Claude Street) with performances by regulars Nari Tomassetti, Ratty Scurvics, the Mudlark Puppets, and burlesque aerialist Ooops the Clown. If not an X-rated Halloween performance, The Allways Lounge is at least a solid R.

If you seek regular old trick-or-treating, the best area is State Street in Uptown. The street is lined with very wealthy people who take Halloween very seriously. Some of the front yards have movie set–quality decorations. The most highly regarded is the Bone House on 6000 St. Charles Street at State. Each year, the owners, Darryl and Louellen Berger, make up fresh wordplay and puns (Die Hard Saints Fan, Napoleon Bone Apart, Bone Appétit, Saturday Night Femur) to attach as signage hung on their seemingly endless supply of plastic skeletons. They receive, on average, 1,200 trick-or-treaters each year.

If you are more seriously or deliriously into vampires or voodoo, Halloween offers signature events.

The Endless Night Vampire Ball, held at the House of Blues each Halloween, is part of a series of masquerade balls produced by Father Sebastiaan. Father Sebastiaan is perhaps the biggest personality in the current vampire subculture. He is the grandson of an orthodontist and nephew of a dentist. Sebastiaan got his first pair of fangs in November 1993, and a year later, he picked up his late grandfather's dental tools and began his career as a fangsmith, with his first customer being his mother. Since then he has traveled the world, handcrafting custom fangs, and is unquestionably the world's most famous master fangsmith. He is also an avid lover of vampire mythology, steampunk, wolves, history, 19th-century art, French culture, ancient Egypt, psychology, and philosophy.

The Bone House   Sabree Hill

His first Vampire Ball was in New York in 1996. There are now balls that have been described as a Venetian masquerade ball mixed with a vampire court, the energy of a rock concert, and the elegance of a burlesque cabaret, in New York, New Orleans, Paris, and Germany. TripAdvisor rated the New Orleans Endless Night Ball the #1 Big Halloween Party in the world. I normally wouldn't trust a word typed onto TripAdvisor, but in this case I must agree.

The Anne Rice Vampire Ball, established by her fan club, is exclusively a New Orleans event. The idea for the ball was hatched in 1988 when founders Suzie Quiroz, Susie Miller, and Teresa Simmons, stood in line for two hours at deVille Bookstore to have Anne Rice sign their books.

I actually attended the inaugural ball, ate from the cakes decorated to look like her book covers, made a little speech, and presented Anne with a real skull that had pronounced canines. Later, I went off into the night following the ball with a few attendees. We ended up at a dark and loud Goth bar on Decatur Street, where one of my new friends took a small vial from around her neck and drew an X on the palm of my hand in what she said was human blood. But that's a story for another time (and one I'd just as soon forget).

Each year the ball now draws around 1,500 people, all elaborately made up, I would say "for the occasion," but when I asked one attendee where she got her fabulous fangs, she replied, "At my dentist." She'd had them bonded to her real teeth, so she was a 24/7 vampire before, during, and after the Vampire Ball. The location changes each year; you can check out the upcoming venue at www.arvlfc.com.

The Undead Con is an outgrowth from Anne Rice's Vampire Ball. It is a weekend of panel discussions, book signings, a cemetery picnic, and the Bizarre Bazaar (vendors displaying vampire-appropriate goods and services) built around the Vampire Ball centerpiece. Both conference and ball are run by Suzie Quiroz, one of the founders of the Anne Rice Fan Club, director of the Vampire Ball, and formerly the longtime assistant for Anne, back when Anne lived in New Orleans. The Undead Con aspires to be the Comic-Con for vampires, but with an emphasis on providing writing skills, marketing strategies, and publishing insights to aspiring horror and gothic writers. Past speakers have included Charlaine Harris, Heather Graham, Laurell K. Hamilton, Sherrilyn Kenyon, and, of course Anne and Christopher Rice.

With three Easter Parades, it's not shocking that New Orleans has more than just the two vampire balls on Halloween. The Anba Dlo Halloween Festival at the Healing Center grows closer to being a decade-old event. The night includes an early-evening parade starting at Mimi's in the Marigny, followed by psychic readings, face painting, and complimentary massage, plus performances deep into the night by first-rate musicians like Jon Mooney and Little Freddie King, with a little burlesque and acrobatics thrown in for good pleasure. Profits from Anba Dlo go to support low-income residents with education and health care.

Hosts of Halloween is a 30-years-and-running party geared toward GLBT participants. All monies collected go to provide funding for Project Lazarus, a home in New Orleans for men and women with AIDS. Hosts of Halloween has raised over $4.6M for Project Lazarus. And, like any good gay party, the spectacle is a little more spectacular. Ordinary costume competitions are turned into thematic krewes. Groups wear similar outfits, like the Puppy Breath Krewe (men carrying large bones, wearing dog ears, and little else) or a Joan Rivers Who Wore It Better? tribute as 15 to 20 men squeeze into the same hideously garish dress and teased wigs.

Now, if you're into both vampires and zombies, you'll have some hard choice to make each Halloween. In addition to the Anne Rice Vampire Ball,

The annual Zombie Run

the Endless Night Ball, and others listed, there's also Voodoo Fest, sponsored by Voodoo Authentica (612 Dumaine Street). Voodoo Fest is a free annual festival that celebrates, hopes to educate, and preserve voodoo traditions in New Orleans.

Here, both local practitioners, like Belfazaar Ashantison, Jesse Brunet, and Doctor Glover, as well as Haitian priestesses like Mama Lola and Mambo Maggie, conduct lectures, book signings, music (musician and historian Sunpie does drumming demonstrations), and perform rituals (for healing not hexing).

You can get your zombie fix at two other events, neither held on nor near Halloween.

The Zombie Run: Extreme is a mud-filled 5K obstacle course each July. In addition to climbing over walls, under tunnels, and up ropes, the #1 obstacle is a horde of flesh-eating zombies. Runners will have three life flags attached to their waist at the start of the run. If you make it to the finish line with at least one flag still attached, you win absolutely nothing. But you should end up feeling more self-confident that if there ever really is a doomsday, postnuclear, end-of-the-world apocalypse (with zombies), you have a solid chance of surviving.

By contacting info@thezombierun.com you can sign up either as a runner or a zombie. Free makeovers and zombie training are provided for the latter.

The Zombie Pub Crawl takes place each June. The pub crawl is a night of zombie-themed bar hopping. Hundreds of undead friends will stagger and shuffle from bar to bar. In addition to killing brain cells, the pub crawl is also helps the lives of animals in need by partnering with the Louisiana and Jefferson SPCAs. You can register at nolazombi.com. Tickets are $20 in advance, $35 day of crawling.

Fangtasia is a relatively new springtime vampire ball, started in 2010 and held from 9:00 P.M. to 5:00 A.M. at the incomparable One Eyed Jacks, a former movie theater, then burlesque house, now music venue with three bars. The first bar looks like a Russian Tea Room with chandeliers and red velvet embossed wallpaper, the second bar is an oval island in the back room with the performance stage, and the third bar upstairs is decorated with matador lamps and velvet Elvis paintings and looks down on the first-floor festivities.

The provocatively named Nyctophilia's Annual Mirror Masquerade is even newer. Just two years old, the July event is a live music and DJs dance at the Dragon's Den (435 Esplanade).

For the more unwholesome wayfarer, make sure you don't rush home right after Halloween. The Day of the Dead, or Día de Muertos, is a Mexican holiday that focuses on gatherings to remember and pray for friends and family members who have died. It's held on what is also All Saints' Day, November 1. The holiday can be traced back to the Aztecs, making the observance some 2,500 years old and counting. In Mexico, traditions include building private altars, called *ofrendas*, to honor the deceased, using sugar skulls, marigolds, and the once favorite food and drink of the departed. Families visit graves to leave these items as gifts. In New Orleans, it's one more reason to dress up, parade, and party.

Our national/local holiday is, of course, Mardi Gras. Every Mardi Gras morning begins (very) early with the North Side Skull & Bone Gang's waking the dead and the living to another Fat Tuesday. Members are dressed in homemade outfits of oversize, papier-mâché skulls (they make a new skull each year), white-painted bones on black clothing, and an apron painted with the words "You're Next!"

Beginning at 5:00 A.M., they troll the neighborhoods, starting at the Backstreet Cultural Museum in Treme (1116 Henriette Delille Place, across from St. Augustine Church) through the Marigny and Bywater, ringing doorbells and banging on every available annoying noise maker from metal trash can lids to dragging chains and manhole covers.

Led by Chief Bruce "Sunpie" Smith, they are following a tradition begun in 1819 that nearly died out before Sunpie's inspiration and efforts. "What we do is in the real spirit of Mardi Gras, we think; a sort of shedding of the flesh," Sunpie explained, adding that it's one way "people give honor to the family spirits that went before them."

The Skeleton Krewe is almost a rival bone gang, without animosity. It was founded in 1999 by self-taught painter, print maker, photographer, and papier-mâché sculptor Christopher Kirsch. Like the North Side Skull & Bone Gang, his krewe was inspired by the early days of Carnival. Kirsch reflected in an interview with Jeff Gonzales on inthenola.com,

> I was reading about Mardi Gras' history. I started reading about Comus. When Comus first started parading, before they had floats, before they had all that, their very first parade in New Orleans, they had these huge papier-mâché heads that they imported from France. Well, I got to thinking about my childhood and in particular, this Abbott and Costello flick, *Abbott and Costello Go to Mars*. In the movie they had all these papier-mâché characters and there was my first epiphany. As I was continuing my research deeper into the origins of Mardi Gras. I started reading about the Bone Gangs of Treme. They date back nearly two hundred years and along with the Indians, they would dress up in skeletal costumes and try to scare the neighborhood kids into staying on the right track. I just thought that was a really great idea.

The Skeleton Krewe has grown to become one of New Orleans' premier marching clubs. It can be seen leading Le Krewe D'Etat Parade Friday night before Mardi Gras and marching from Uptown to downtown very early Mardi Gras morning.

Both the Skeleton Krewe and the North Side Skull & Bone Gang are currently full and not accepting new members. Doesn't mean you can't make your own papier-mâché head or start your own krewe.

ANNIE FENN

CHAPTER 9

Assorted Mayhem—
Chopped Up and
Served Fresh Here

Basically, New Orleans is an amusement park where you can get killed. —James Franco

I like to tell people I have the heart of a small boy. Then, I tell them it's in a jar on my desk. —**Robert Bloch, author of *Psycho***

This chapter is for all those odds and bitter ends that didn't fit elsewhere. If you steadfastly refuse to believe in vampires and ghosts, this is the "real" stuff that'll make you ask, "Is it safe to walk around?" and "Where should I *not* go?"

Like all cities, from Fall River, Massachusetts, and its most famous citizen Lizzie Borden, to San Francisco, where Fatty Arbuckle crushed Virginia Rappe in the throes of passion, New Orleans also has its share of gruesome or bizarre death scenes. Faced with competition from voodoo and vampires, ours sometimes suffer from lack of attention. As was the case with ghost stories, there are just too many to be covered in a lone chapter. My attempt is to recount just the juiciest.

Love 'Em and Cleave 'Em

Zack Bowen and Addie Hall became media darlings during and just after Katrina as the young couple chose to stay in New Orleans and ride out the hurricane. She was a bartender at the Spotted Cat; Zack was a bartender at Buffa's. Without electricity, they cooked meals on a hibachi or trash tin in front of their apartment stoop on Governor Nicholls Street. Whenever they had pressing needs, Addie would flash her bare boobs and the police were sure to stop and help. Numerous articles appeared about this fun and quintessentially New Orleans couple.

However, as the city slowly pulled itself back together in the months following Katrina, Zack slowly began to fall apart. He was a Gulf War veteran and, in retrospect, clearly suffered from PTSD. A year after the flood, the two had been evicted from the Governor Nicholls apartment and had moved to another at 826 N. Rampart Street, above the New Orleans Voodoo Spiritual Temple.

On the night of October 16, 2006, Bowen had been out drinking with friends. He appeared to others to be in good spirits and talked about how much he needed a vacation. The next night he took his vacation, leaping off the top of the Omni Royal Orleans Hotel. Cigarette burns covered his body. A suicide note was tucked in his pants pocket:

> I didn't contact any of my family, so that'll explain the shock. This is not accidental. I had to take my own life to pay for the one I took … Every last one of these I failed at, hence the 28 cigarette burns, one for each year of my existence.

The suicide note also directed the police to Bowen's apartment, where he had spray-painted his ex-wife's telephone number on the wall for her to be notified of his death. Another spray-painted note pointed to a couple of large pots on top of the stove. Inside one they found the head of Addie Hall; in the other were her hands and feet. A basting pan inside the oven contained her arms and legs—one leg had been sprinkled with Cajun seasonings. There were chopped vegetables in a container on top of the stove.

When the police opened Addie's journal, Zack had written more details:

> Today is Monday 16 October, 2:00 AM. I killed her at 1:00 AM, Thursday, 5 October. I very calmly strangled her. It was very quick.

His note claimed he had repeatedly had sex with her corpse after killing her. The following day, he took her body into the bathroom and began to dismember her with a handsaw. Police noted that he had attempted to clean up the bathroom.

He put the thermostat on 60 degrees to cut down on decomposition and smell and for 10 days went about his routine business in the outside world. I should think returning each day to an apartment with a hacked-up lover would be worse than coming back to one who pecks at you, "Where have you been? Who were you with?"

Zack's diary entry continued,

> Halfway through the task, I stopped and thought about what I was doing. The decision to halt the first idea and move to Plan B (the crime scene you are now in) came after awhile. I scared myself not only by the action of calmly strangling the woman I've loved for one and a half years, but by my entire lack of remorse. I've known forever how horrible a person I am (ask anyone).

There was no evidence found in the autopsy performed on Zack's body or on Addie's remains that he'd actually eaten any of her, so it's not like he was all that bad.

If you're thinking about touring the home, you can't. Someone lives there today, and I'm quite sure the tenant wouldn't take kindly to morbid tourist visitors' knocking on the door. Hard to imagine living in Zack and Addie's old apartment, though. I'd at least want a replacement stove.

A Hatchet Job(s)

Beginning in 1911, a series of people were found hacked to death by an ax in their home. The first was Cruti, the second Rosetti (killed with his wife), and the third was named Schiambra (also killed with his wife). All three cases involved the murder of an owner of an Italian grocery. All had a pattern by which an incredibly small panel had been hacked through the door to gain entry. Without even considering a little person or dwarf who had an unnatural hatred for sopressata or mascarpone, the police immediately thought they were dealing with the Mafia. Perhaps the victims had not paid "dues" or failed to meet loan payback deadlines.

A few Italian citizens of New Orleans requested police protection. Some whispered about an organization called the Black Hand. Organized crime was a dominant force in New Orleans at the time, particularly in the blocks known as Little Palermo. The Black Hand was an alleged secret society of enforcers.

The ax murders suddenly stopped, only to return seven years later. On May 23, 1918, another Italian grocer, this one named Joseph Maggio, and his wife were butchered, while sleeping in their apartment above the Maggio grocery store. Again, a small entry hole had been cut into the back door.

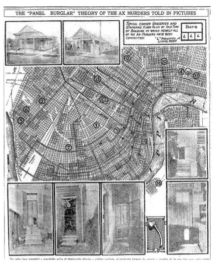

Just two weeks later, a bread man didn't find grocery store owner Louis Besumer up early and waiting for morning deliveries, as was his usual pattern. When the delivery-man went around to the side door, Besumer came out covered in blood. Besumer said that someone had

"The Axeman of New Orleans" was followed closely by the local papers

attacked him and pointed toward the bedroom. Inside, Besumer's mistress was in the bed, covered with a blood-soaked sheet.

A local newspaper, the *States*, ran with the story that the Axeman had returned to New Orleans. The paper speculated about the killer, wondering whether he was a fiend, a madman, a robber, a sadist, or some supernatural entity. People were terrified. A killer was at large who managed to break into people's homes while they slept. Reported sightings all over the city flooded the police offices. One even had the Axeman wandering around as a man dressed in woman's clothing.

Next was Steve Boca, again a New Orleans grocer. He stumbled from his home to a neighbor's house on Elysian Fields Avenue with ax wounds to his skull.

On September 2, a druggist named William Carlson heard a noise at his back door as he was reading late at night. He got his revolver, called out several times, then fired through the door. When he went outside, no one was there, but the police found hacks on the door panels, where someone was trying to gain entry.

Then the assaults stopped again for the rest of the year. New Orleans settled into its normal routines. Months went by without a report of the Axeman. People wondered if he might have left the area. World War I ended and New Orleanians got distracted by other matters. They were soon to find out their assumptions about the Axeman being gone were wrong.

The newspaper received a letter dated, "Hell, March 13, 1919." It read:

Esteemed Mortal:

They have never caught me and they never will. They have never seen me, for I am invisible, even as the ether that surrounds your earth. I am not a human being, but a spirit and a fell demon from the hottest hell. I am what you Orleanians and your foolish police call the Axeman.

When I see fit, I shall come again and claim other victims. I alone know who they shall be. I shall leave no clue except my bloody axe, besmeared with the blood and brains of him whom I have sent below to keep me company.

If you wish you may tell the police not to rile me. Of course I am a reasonable spirit. I take no offense at the way they have conducted their investigation in the past. In fact, they have been so utterly stupid as to amuse not only me but His Satanic Majesty, Francis Josef, etc. But tell them to beware. Let them not try to discover what I am, for it were better that they were never born than to incur the wrath of the Axeman. I don't think there is any need of such a warning, for I feel sure the police will always dodge me, as they have in the past. They are wise and know how to keep away from all harm.

Undoubtedly, you Orleanians think of me as a most horrible murderer, which I am, but I could be much worse if I wanted to. If I wished, I could pay a visit to your city every night. At will I could slay thousands of your best citizens, for I am in close relationship to the Angel of Death.

Now, to be exact, at 12:15 (earthly time) on next Tuesday night, I am going to visit New Orleans again. In my infinite mercy, I am going to make a proposition to you people. Here it is:

I am very fond of jazz music, and I swear by all the devils in the nether regions that every person shall be spared in whose home a jazz band is in full swing at the time I have mentioned. If everyone has a jazz band going, well, then, so much the better for you people. One thing is certain and that is that some of those people who do not jazz it on Tuesday night (if there be any) will get the axe.

Well, as I am cold and crave the warmth of my native Tartarus, and as it is about time that I leave your earthly home, I will cease my discourse. Hoping that thou wilt publish this, and that it may go well with thee, I have been, am and will be the worst spirit that ever existed either in fact or realm of fantasy.

The Axeman

Even if it was a prank, people took the letter seriously. The night of March 19, the whole city sounded like Bourbon Street, or what Bourbon Street used to sound like back then, with jazz blaring from every door. No one was murdered that night.

There were to be two more victims. A young woman named Sarah Laumann, neither Italian nor a grocer, was struck in the face by an ax. She survived the attack with some cuts, the loss of several teeth, and a concussion, but she could recall for the police no details of her attacker.

October 27, 1919, was to be the Axeman's farewell act. Early that morning, Mrs. Mike Pepitone, the wife of a grocer, awoke to hear a struggle in the next room where her husband slept. She reached the door just in time to see a shadowy man disappear through a door on the opposite side. Mike Pepitone lay in his blood-soaked bed. He had been butchered with blood and bits splattered on the walls, ceiling, and floor.

And just like that, the Axeman was gone. He was never seen or heard from in the city again. His crimes would remain unsolved and no one would ever learn his true identity. Sorry to disappoint you if you're a *Criminal Minds* fan and need a tidy conclusion.

Father Decomposes Best

A solitary murder makes the cut and into this chapter because it involves a priest and wanton sex. Always a fun combination.

The Chateau Le Moyne Hotel, owned by Holiday Inn, is described online as a "family-friendly hotel." On March 24, 1998, it was anything but. A housekeeper walked in to clean a guest's room and discovered a man's body on the floor, facedown between the two beds. He was naked except for a pair of socks (so obviously not a vampire, or the left sock would be missing). The floor, the walls, the bedspreads were all splattered with blood.

Tourism is the lifeblood of New Orleans. When a tourist gets murdered, in the French Quarter, in a family-friendly hotel, it becomes a high-priority case. The crime scene was a mess. Mingled with the body and the blood were sex toys and condoms scattered everywhere around the room.

The cause of death was quite clear. The victim had been stabbed many, many times. Said Dr. Frank Minyard, the longtime New Orleans coroner (so, he must have seen oodles of carnage over the years), "It was a horrible, horrible scene. There were so many stab wounds I couldn't count them all. There was blood on the walls, on the bedroom floor, on the bathroom floor, all over the place. It was horrible."

The case went from gruesome to a potentially notorious when the body was identified as Ramon Martinez, a Catholic priest. When he was seven years old, Martinez had fled Castro's Cuba with his family and settled near New Orleans. As an adult, he moved to Los Angeles with the ambition to be an actor.

Martinez's first taste of acting was a role as a delivery boy in *The Gingerbread Lady*, starring Vera Miles. He then landed roles in the television sitcoms *Archie Bunker's Place*, *Three's Company*, *Diff'rent Strokes*, *Lois & Clark*, and the daytime soap opera *General Hospital*.

Someplace along the way, Ramon met the Catholic archbishop of Los Angeles, himself a former actor. Guided by the archbishop, Ramon returned to New Orleans and enrolled in Notre Dame Seminary. In 1989, he graduated with a master's degree in divinity and was ordained a priest in the Archdiocese of New Orleans.

On the fateful night, Father Ramon registered under his own name and listed his address as a post office box in the town of Port Sulphur, a small town 50 miles south of New Orleans, where he served as pastor of St. Patrick's Church. At some point he picked up a French Quarter street hustler—the wrong street hustler, as it turned out. Robert Chidester, in his confession, claimed he agreed to oral sex, but when Ramon tried to bend him over and sodomize him, the young hustler was repulsed. He pulled out a double-edged knife, which he just happened to be carrying, and to defend himself against Ramon's sexual attack, he plunged his knife into the priest . . . over 40 times.

Right after the murder, Chidester fled to Cincinnati. Maybe he'd heard Mark Twain's quote, "When the world comes to an end, I want to be in Cincinnati. Everything gets there ten years later."

While Chidester was trying to keep a low profile, Father Ramon's profile was taking a few hits. Investigators uncovered more than three hundred pornographic movies and a couple hundred skin magazines and books in the priest's residence. The police did what they could to minimize the damage to the priest's reputation. After the murder, the *Times-Picayune* carried no mention that Ramon was nude when the housekeeper discovered his body. There was no mention of sex toys. No mention of used condoms. No mention of three hundred porno movies.

Chidester proved not to be gifted at keeping a low profile. During his stay in Cincinnati, he wandered across the Ohio River into Kentucky and stabbed someone else. He was released for lack of evidence and for lack of willingness to prosecute by the victim. Then he displayed even less smarts by returning to New Orleans and hooking up with a tarot card reader. During pillow talk, Chidester tried to impress his new lover by telling her that he'd murdered a Catholic priest. As a token of his love, Chidester gave her the knife he'd used to kill the priest. Quite the romantic!

Seeing him as at least a deadbeat boyfriend and possibly a beat-her-to-death boyfriend, she turned him in. On the evening of September 24, 1998, detectives crashed into Robert Chidester's flophouse apartment at 2121 Jena Street and arrested him. In his confession, he claimed to be an angel of death sent to punish the wicked priest.

Even after solving the high-profile case, police officials were reluctant to release any details and avoided mentioning sex. Lt. Robert McNeil, commander of the Homicide Division, would say only that Ramon and Chidester argued. "We have some idea what they were arguing about," he told the *Times-Picayune*. "But it would be inappropriate for me to disclose that at this time."

Rather than the death penalty, the presiding judge sentenced Chidester to 25 years in prison, and thanked him for sparing everyone what had promised to be a remarkably sordid trial.

Love Means Never Being Able to Say You're Sorry

Dr. Etienne Deschamps had been born in France, studied to be a dentist, but remade himself when he migrated to New Orleans and peddled his revolutionary "Magnetic Physiology." This new science from Paris claimed to cure all maladies by magnetism, up to and including erectile dysfunction. Outside his home at 714 St. Peter Street, his shingle read (in French): "Searching for truth? Doing it well?" Etienne also passed out business cards on street corners with his slogan (in French): "Let us look for the truth! Let us do good! Let us be magnetized!"

With his advertising, his charm, and good looks (a whole lot more attractive than Dr. Oz), Dr. Des had no trouble building up a client base. These were less educated, more gullible times than our current oxygen bar, Q-ray ionized bracelet, Botox, and colon-cleansing one.

According to Deschamps, his magnetic powers could do far more than just heal what ailed you. Magnetic Physiology, or MP, also gave one psychic powers. His MP goal was to find the lost treasure of Jean Lafitte. There were stories of an enormous treasure buried by Lafitte somewhere in the Barataria Swamp, where his pirates used to hide out and where today you can take airboat tours and feed marshmallows to alligators.

Dr. Des said he needed a 12-year-old virgin to act as the medium to help locate the buried treasure. No explanation was given as to why a 12-year-old virgin. But, it just so happened, one of his best repeat customers, Jules Deitsch, had a 12-year-old daughter, presumed to be virginal, and she just happened to be extremely beautiful.

Dr. Des suggested that Jules's daughter, Juliette, would be perfect. Both he and her father could become wealthy beyond their dreams after the treasure was located. Deitsch fell for the plan and agreed to let Juliette participate. What could go wrong?

The plan involved Deschamps' dosing Juliette with liberal amounts of chloroform to open up her mind to psychic influences during their very private "mediumship" sessions. No alarm bells went off because (a) chloroform was new and any ill effects of its unregulated use were not yet known, (b) Dr. Des was a doctor, after all, with an MP degree, and (c) Jules Deitsch was a total fucking idiot.

On January 30, 1889, what probably seems inevitable happened. Dr. Des asked Juliette to strip naked, as he often did, and then he stripped down and got into bed with her for their "psychic session." He used a handkerchief over her mouth to dose Juliette with chloroform. Needing an extra hit, he got out of bed and dressed himself, and went to buy more chloroform.

Juliette's younger sister, who'd witnessed all of this, used his departure as a chance to run home. When she rushed back with her dad, they found Juliette and the doctor in bed, both naked, with her head on his chest. Juliette was dead. Deschamps was still alive, though he had stabbed himself in the chest four times. The coroner, Y. R. LeMonnier, conducted an autopsy on Juliette's body and determined the cause of death was an overdose of chloroform. There were clear burn marks on her lips from the drug as well as evidence that Juliette had been sexually abused over a long period of time.

As for Etienne Deschamps, his wounds were superficial. He was removed from the Charity Hospital to the Parish Prison. While in prison, he also made grandiose claims that he could find Lafitte's treasure if only he could be released and that the authorities had no right to keep him locked up since he was a scientist and a great man.

Deschamps' arraignment became quite a spectacle. He protested that putting him on trial in an English-speaking court was a farce since he only spoke French, that he was incapable of murder because he was a gentleman, and that the entire trial was an attempt to smear the "fair name of France."

He was found guilty after the jury deliberated a full 18 minutes. At a retrial, the new jury took 13 minutes before finding him guilty.

As Etienne Deschamps awaited his execution, he became more bizarre. Guards observed him in his cell having extended conversations with Juliette and Jean Lafitte, although witnesses were divided whether this was due to insanity or an attempt to feign insanity to avoid execution. When the execution date was set, Deschamps protested that he would be hanged alongside other "common" prisoners. Being a refined French gentleman, this seemed like the ultimate indignity. The French consul even filed a complaint to the governor and lieutenant governor.

Governor Nicholls, facing complaints from both sides, was as thoroughly sick of the case as everybody else. He set a new execution date on May 12, 1892. This time, Etienne Deschamps was finally hanged as scheduled, loudly proclaiming his innocence to the very end. "Adieu. I am innocent. LeMonnier is the criminal."

If You Have Time on Your Bloody Hands

If your return flight gets canceled and you're stuck an extra day here (there are worse places to be stuck than New Orleans), you might want to venture out to 4500 Magazine Street. It's currently the home of Zen Pet Retail & Grooming. The nondescript store you find there may not make the hair on your arms stand on end, but the door that once graced the entrance will.

When Nine Inch Nails front man Trent Reznor lived in New Orleans, he set up his private record label, Nothing Studio, at the space where Zen Pet now stands. The studio specialized in industrial rock and electronic music, releasing albums by 2WO, Pig, Pop Will Eat Itself, 12 Rounds, the Meat Beat Manifesto, Einstürzende Neubauten, and one you've actually heard of, Marilyn Manson.

In designing Nothing Studio, Trent brought the front door from his old studio at 10050 Cielo Drive near Beverly Hills. That had been the home where Charles Manson and family butchered Sharon Tate and four others. The front door still had the word "Pig" written by Susan Atkins in Sharon Tate's blood. I don't recognize any of the current doors on Magazine as being the door. It's possible the holistic pet people didn't know they possessed a morbidly revered object and the door got tossed in some dumpsite.

Everyone Out of the Pool! Well . . . Except You

To end this chapter on a cheerier note, I'm going to forgo mentioning the more twisted and bloody tales.

Instead, let's talk about a pool party. The September 1985 party that was being held to celebrate the first summer in memory without a single drowning in a New Orleans municipal pool. To honor the occasion, more than two hundred people gathered. Unfortunately, as the party was breaking up, they found a fully dressed body on the bottom of the deep end. Jerome Moody spoiled the summer's perfect record by drowning at a party with four lifeguards on duty and more than two hundred off-duty lifeguards in attendance.

MIKELL HERRICH

CHAPTER 10

Crypt Adviser

This final chapter will tell you where to take ghost tours, partake of tarot or psychic readings, and purchase talismans to take home with you. Please don't go home without your Smudging Stick or Obsidian Scrying Orb. The former you're supposed to light. The smoke filling your room will cleanse, relax, and banish bad juju. The latter is a crystal ball made from volcanic glass, used since the time of Nostradamus, and said to be absolutely premium in contacting spirits and revealing hidden knowledge.

It is impossible to be comprehensive in this chapter. We have more ghost tours and voodoo shops than New York has pizza parlors or Los Angeles has taco stands. I hope at least to be helpful.

Don't Drink and Revive: Ghost Tours

Following are (some of) New Orleans' ghost, vampire, and voodoo tours. You have over 20 tours to choose from. Many of them are lurking in the shadows, ready to snatch your $25 and give you a ghastly rather than ghostly experience. A simple rule for ghost tours: be careful, as the more you drink, the more ghosts you'll see.

When I first moved to New York City, I went into Central Park on a beautiful Sunday and strolled by the Loeb Boathouse. The lake was so jammed with rented boats it most resembled a huge, water-based, bumper car ride. This activity is considered relaxing leisure time in New York, where residents are used to spending two hours a day in rush-hour traffic to get from Houston Street to the Holland Tunnel (i.e., four blocks).

The French Quarter each night between 7:00 P.M. and 10:00 P.M. feels very much like the pond in Central Park as group after group of tourists cluster, three guides deep, in front the LaLaurie Mansion and the Jean Lafitte Bar.

Big Easy Tours

(800) 301-3184

www.BigEasyTours.us

Big Easy seems to be a smorgasbord of every kind of tour from swamp to city. I list it here because it offers a Scandal Tour, described on site as "Murder, Mayhem, Corruption, Adultery, Prostitution, Assassination, Extortion, Mafia and Conspiracy. This is the most shocking twisted history tour of America's original sin city! Your tour guides will hold nothing back as they take you into the darkest places of the city's most secret history."

Bloody Mary Tours

941 Bourbon St.

(504) 523-7684

www.bloodymarystours.com

Bloody Mary is like the Court of Two Sisters of ghost tours. Two Sisters has over 80 items on its brunch menu. Bloody Mary's menu of tours is likewise extensive. You can choose from the Haunted Pub Crawl; Cities of the Dead 3-Pac cemetery tour; Saints & Sinners (3 churches and 2 cemeteries); New Orleans After Dark Ghost Town tour; a Bachelorette Party or Honeymoon Outing, called "romantic with a voodoo twist"; the Magical Mystery Tour; haunted dinners; the Paranormal Adventure Tour with automatic writing, folk magic, past lives, spirit guides, and a séance, plus a standard cemetery tour; and then Bloody Mary's most popular and signature tour, the Moonlight Graveyard Tour, the only nighttime cemetery tour offered in New Orleans.

Bloody Mary herself is as much of the story as our burial or voodoo practices. Born and raised as a "Delta Babe," her Louisiana bloodlines trace back to the founding of New Orleans in 1718. *Southern Woman* magazine drenched her in nicknames: "the Cultural Diva," "the Ultimate Insider" and "the Poet Priestess of the Spirit of New Orleans," "a true spokeswoman of her hometown," and "an elegant, modern southern belle."

French Quarter History & Ghostbuster Tours

622 Pirates Alley
(504) 561-8687
www.frenchquarterhistorytours.com

I'm ready to give this tour company a better blurb whenever it figures out what it really wants to be. Its website directs you to its Facebook page to find out the times of its tours—for some reason not made available on the website. Its sales brochures have information blacked out with marking pen.

CRYPT ADVISOR

Its presentation, on one hand, emphasizes the appropriateness of its entertaining-for-kids stories. Facebook highlights include a seven-year-old girl; a copied Yelp comment focuses on a 10-year-old boy. But then, trying to be all things for all people, it ditches the stories and pitches its techno-glitzy use of EMF detectors and Laser Temp guns.

FQH&GBT pushes its low prices, but the $25 price tag is identical to and not a penny cheaper than every other ghost tour. And it closes the deal by clumsily merging *X-Files* and *Ghostbusters* with "They are waiting for you to find them. Who you gonna call?" I think I will call a tour where I don't have to work so hard just to know what time it starts.

French Quarter Phantoms

718 N Rampart St. (inside the Voodoo Lounge)
(504) 666-8300
www.frenchquarterphantoms.com

French Quarter Phantoms claims, "We are not the biggest—WE ARE THE BEST! This is NOT your Ordinary Cheap Thrill!!" Its hook is that it hires and trains über-smart tour guides, or, as the company calls them, "Master Storytellers." Its website states its guides are "are very well educated, having earned degrees in History, Forensic Anthropology, Music, Education, Literature and Theater."

The website goes on to state, repeatedly, that the tour guides give "*historically accurate* ghost and vampire tales," adding you can expect "a *historically accurate* fun-filled tour," and you are invited to "Join us on our walking tour for *historically accurate* tales."

Just in case you haven't gotten the message, the customer endorsements include the comments of twotoedsloth of Silver Spring, Maryland: "This company seems to place a very high value on *research*, preferring to tell *true stories* and let the *history* do the talking."

For historical accuracy, I must add that everyone I have met from French Quarter Phantoms, from owner Cindi Richardson, to tour manager Sandy Hester, to tour guide and busty model for FQF brochures and side-of-streetcar ads Hope Kodman, have all been engaging and delightful.

They are also one of only two companies that give tours of Treme, which is only the most historically important African American neighborhood in America.

Ghost Expeditions
(504) 582-6991
itunes.apple.com

This is a downloadable tour app with the ease and comfort to take the tour whenever you want, at any pace you desire, with whomever you want to join. Of course, you'll have more luck getting your questions answered by Siri on your phone than a Ghost Expeditions app.

My bigger concern comes from its claim that the guide "provides researched information to debunk the most fantastic of Big Easy ghost legends including tour favorites like the tortuous Madame Lalaurie and her haunted Royal Street Mansion, Julie the Quadroon Mistress, and the bloody massacre at the Sultan's House to name a few." That sounds dreadful, like taking a ghost tour with a recorded script by an old curmudgeon like Simon Cowell or John Boehner as your nay-saying, debunking guide. Who really wants that?

Gray Line Tours
(504) 569-1401
Meet at the Natchez Lighthouse behind Jax Brewery
www.graylineneworleans.com

To the good, Gray Line's Ghost Tour is the only one that's worked out a deal to enter the Bourbon Orleans Hotel, where a ghost, the Lady in Red, hangs out in the second-floor ballroom. There's also a glass display booth on the first floor where you can see an antique vampire kit, once considered as much as a must-have item to be stored in the house as Band-Aids and dental floss.

To the inexplicable, this is the only ghost tour that refuses to go by the LaLaurie Mansion. Gray Line Tours designer Etienne explained to me the reason for skipping the most haunted house in New Orleans in a manner that ended up making about as much sense as Yogi Berra's famous quote about a New York restaurant, "Nobody goes there anymore. It's too crowded."

Haunted History Tours

(504) 861-2727

Meet in front of Reverend Zombie's Voodoo Shop, 723 St. Peter St.

www.neworleansghosttour.com and www.hauntedhistorytours.com

While every tour listed on these pages claims to be #1, for those who like to stick to "stubborn things" (facts), Sidney Smith's Haunted History Tours is far and away the most popular. It is also among the most venerable. Sidney bought back the rights and images for his first company, New Orleans Ghost Tours. So, if you're wondering which tour would be better, Haunted History or New Orleans Ghost Tours, that's like choosing between Patty and Cathy on *The Patty Duke Show*. That reference will only make sense for readers over 50.

Sidney's expressed desire is to have his tour guides be entertaining and good storytellers, but not overly chewing-up-the-scenery, theatrical in costume/presentation. His website's description "*mildly* theatrical, hugely historical, and thoroughly entertaining" is a muffled shot at former employee, Lord Chaz, who's anything but mild. The site's phrase "Step beyond the *gray line* of reality into New Orleans' true haunted history" is a more overt shot.

Haunted History also does a Voodoo Tour and a Vampire Tour.

Historic New Orleans Tours

(504) 407-2120

tour@tourneworleans.com

The company is owned and run by Robert Florence, a noted historian who has appeared on many TV and radio programs, including CBS News's *Travels with Harry*, NPR's *Pulse of the Planet*, and the History Channel's *Modern Marvels*, explaining New Orleans cemeteries, and who has contributed to several documentaries, articles, and museum exhibits regarding the culture of south Louisiana.

He employs one of the most sought-after tour guides, Karen Jefferies. She owns the haunted Dauphine House (1830 Dauphine Street) and has been a paranormal investigator with over 15 years' experience. Karen's tours will combine her deep knowledge of our haunted history with stories of her own paranormal experiences.

Livery

(504) 561-1000
Meet at Jax Brewery Bistro, 620 Decatur St.
www.liverytours.com

If you Google "ghost tours new orleans," Livery will appear first and exclaim "NOLA's #1 Ghost Tour." By #1, I think it means #1 listed on the Google search page, and that's placement you can buy.

If you need transportation to and from the airport or a private car to get you to an event, I might recommend Livery (though Riverbend Charters would be my #1 choice). As far as ghost tours go, Livery is really good at getting you to and from the airport. Sometimes the traffic on I-10 can be pretty scary.

Lord Chaz

(504) 638-2895
Meet at 718 Bourdon St.
www.lordchaz.com

After multiple careers as a political operative, an electrician, truck driver, door-to-door encyclopedia salesman, and owner of a video store, Lord Chaz moved to New Orleans to be near his daughter, then living with his ex-wife. As happened to so many, New Orleans seduced him and "nudged" him toward what he was meant to be. Now dressed up in top hat, floor-length coat, purple sunglasses, and his signature 6-inch nails, Lord Chaz is a far howl from understated.

Lord Chaz has become an integral part of the New Orleans vampire and Goth scene. He is the Grande Master of Ceremonies and onstage host of several New Orleans annual vampire events, including the Dark Cotillion, Endless Night, Fangtasia, the Mirror Masquerade. He coproduces and performs the Internet podcast show Bite Me! Vampire TV. He has appeared in several movies and numerous television shows, including *Strange Universe*, *America's Best Ghost Stories*, *Haunted America*, and a cameo appearance on the second season of the E Network show *The Girls Next Door*.

He's been prominently featured in the music video *Borderline* by the 69 Eyes as well as a promotional video for the graphic novel *The Curse of the Venus Aversa*.

On a Lord Chaz tour, you come for The Show. His tours are designed to be theatrically over-the-top. He does not call them "tours," but rather "Vampire Street Theater" and he is much more of an entertainer than anything so banal as a tour guide.

Magic Tours
720 St. Louis St.
(504) 588-9693
www.magictoursnola.com

Magic Tours bills itself as "alternative tours for the intelligent traveler." Its guides are professors, historians, and journalists. Website copy positions Magic Tours against the competition: "Some do it passably, other do it embarrassedly. We do it professionally."

Founded in 1992, it is certainly among the oldest and most venerable ghost tour still haunting the sidewalks of the French Quarter. But being among the oldest wouldn't compel me to turn off younger sports franchises like the Miami Heat or Seattle Seahawks in order to watch the centuries-old Chicago Cubs and Cincinnati Reds.

New Orleans Spirit Tours
621 Royal St.
(504) 314-0806
www.neworleanstours.com

This company's tours are $21 rather than $25. Tour guides George, Julia, Adam, and someone named Weezy get praise from tour takers Dawn from Milwaukee, Cyndle from Texarkana, and Doug and Tammy from someplace called Klamath Falls.

Spirit Tours flirts with danger. Its supposed two-hour ghost tour starts at 8:15 P.M., when it risks being ticketed for being out on the street, giving tours, 15 minutes after the 10:00 P.M. curfew. Its 1:15 P.M. cemetery tour has the greater risk of being stuck inside the cemetery after the 3:00 P.M. lockup.

NOLA Ghost Hunting Tours

(504) 708-3567

www.nolaghosthuntingtours.com

NOLA Ghost Hunting Tours is a group of "professional paranormal investigators" that have years of experience, and they have *equipment!* (like EMF meters, thermal cameras, and trigger dolls). More recently, they have the notoriety of a TV show on the SyFy Channel, *Deep South Paranormal.*

Kevin Betzer (profiled in this book) and Chris Melancon (Paranormal Society of New Orleans) don't tell you creepy chestnut stories about New Orleans' past, but essentially put you in the middle of a ghost-hunting show to bring you in direct, firsthand contact with spirits, and not the kind served in plastic to-go cups.

NOLA Ghost Hunting Tours is for people who'd rather go on a safari, with the associated risk being mauled, or possibly worse, roaming around for hours and not finding anything. Other tours may seem are more like scripted sessions going to an orderly zoo or natural history museum.

Nawlins NateScott

(504) 451-7163 or (504) 367-1499

Meet at the front gate of St. Louis #1

islandofalgierstours.web.com

Nawlins NateScott is a person, not a company. Most often he is posted at the front gate of St. Louis #1, like a voodoo version of a Buckingham Palace guard. He's always dressed in all white except for his black top hat. With his Willie Nelson pigtails and gold teeth, he may seem more streetwise than scholarly, but he gets consistent and nearly universal raves on social media sites. Westmickeyhelm from Texas raved "Nawlins NateScott was the best person for this tour. Very informative, very education and at times made it very suspenseful." Colleen from the Hamptons "Nawlins NateScott was wonderful and was full of knowledge and history!! We like to ask lots of questions and he was able to answer all of them!! I highly recommend his tours if you are looking to learn as much as you can about New Orleans and its history." I personally found him delightful, informed, and quite helpful.

He's $5 less expensive than other tours: $20, $15 for four or more people, and kids aged 12 and under are free (with parent). Perhaps best of all, he can adjust to your schedule, giving you one- or two-hour tours and able to guide you anytime the cemetery is open, not the set times of other tours.

Mister Nawlins also does African American history tours and what he calls a "Gumbo" tour.

Save Our Cemeteries

501 Basin St.
(504) 525-3377
www.saveourcemeteries.org

Taking a tour with Save Our Cemeteries (profiled in chapter 2) is like getting a puppy from the ASPCA. You're fulfilling your wants while doing some good. Plus, (I think) Save Our Cemeteries is your one and only option to tour certain cemeteries like St. Louis #2.

Strange True Tours

513 Royal St.
(504) 662-1350
http://strangeneworleans.weebly.com

Strange True Tours bill itself as "the Original Adult Oriented History tour of New Orleans!" The tours are rated PG-13 flirting with R due to adult content, fittingly rough language, and drug use references.

Less about ghosts, Rev. Master Jeffrey covers a wide range of subjects from pirates, prostitutes, cross dressers, dueling stories, hot dogs, funerals, and offers an exclusive Lee Harvey Oswald & JFK Conspiracy Tour.

STT's cemetery tour has been personally endorsed by Daisy Berkowitz. Yeah, I didn't know Daisy, either. It was the stage name of Scott Putsky, a guitar player for Marilyn Manson who left the group about 20 years ago. That'd be like my using Tommy Kirk to endorse *Fear Dat*. Tommy was the star in the 1966 movie *The Ghost in the Invisible Bikini*. I hope I don't now get hater tweets from the Scott Putsky or Tommy Kirk fan clubs.

Voodoo Bone Lady Tours

(504) 267-2040

www.voodooboneladytours.com

The newest addition to the lineup of ghost and voodoo tours is the Voodoo Bone Lady. I have not taken her tours. I base this snotty entry exclusively from my computer screen.

Facebook shows she has amassed 23 "Likes" in two years. This compares to 967 Lord Chaz likes, over 15,000 for Haunted History Tours, and over a million "Likes" for Anne Rice. Her website uses as the #1 tag line "The Voodoo Bone Lady Accurately Predicts the Super Bowl for National TV!" The National TV! turns out to be HLN, a CNN spin-off best known for broadcasting George H. W. Bush died in 1992, when he had merely vomited into the lap of Japanese prime minister Kiichi Miyazawa. The Bone Lady's prediction was that the Ravens would beat the 49ers in the 2012 Super Bowl, held here in New Orleans. ESPN must be a psychic vortex as Tom Jackson, Ron Jaworski, and Mike Golic also predicted a Ravens win. I've always suspected Golic might be into voodoo spells. How else can you explain how this beanbag chair impersonating a man has a prime-time, drive time, radio, and TV gig?

Witches Brew Tours

(504) 413-3120

www.witchesbrewtours.com

The Witches Brew tag line, *"Follow us if you dare,"* is not the most sales inducing I've ever seen. Honda Civic: Buy one if you dare! The Olive Garden: Try our new Alfredo pasta bowl, if you dare!

It continues, "Owner Tamara is rumored to be the reincarnated spirit of Madame Delphine La Laurie, and Tommy has a sordid and dubious history." If you're only in town for a weekend, why not be led around by a sordid dubious guide and a mass murderer? Hey, it's New Orleans, what could possibly go wrong?

Malicious Consumption: Voodoo and Vampire Shops

For all your love potion and chicken feet needs, following are our voodoo and vampire shops. Sadly, I must report the Museum of Necromantic Art and Gallery has closed. My wife and I went into the store, knowing full well what necromancy meant, but figuring that couldn't possibly be what the store was about. But it was. We made a quick exit.

Boutique du Vampyre

709 St. Ann St.
(504) 561-8267

The boutique is the only brick-and-mortar vampire shop in America, and only one of three in the world. It was created and is run by Marita Jaeger, another in a long line of visitors seduced by New Orleans. "When I first came here, I fell in love with the city and never left." The shop is mostly filled with one-of-a-kind treasures made by one of the 130 local artisans she uses. Here you can buy candles, pewter charms, handmade paper, leather journals, a vampire lesson box, vampire perfume made by Hove, a hundred-year-old perfumer on Chartres Street, and hot sauce from Transylvania, Louisiana. The store also has a give-away map of all the gothic shops in the French Quarter.

Erzulie's Authentic Voodoo

807 Royal St.
(504) 525-2055

The shop says it's authentic right in its name, so it must be, right? It has another location in Providence, Rhode Island, making Erzulie's an authentic voodoo chain store.

The New Orleans location underwent a serious upgrade when it brought in Kalila Katherina Smith, voodoo, vampire, ghost expert, and storyteller. It offers love spells, voodoo spells, and voodoo love spells, plus magic spells, voodoo dolls, goat's milk voodoo soaps, anointing oils, perfumes, voodoo dolls, and psychic readings . . . pretty much everything you'd expect from a voodoo shop. It also has voodoo apps for your iPhone or Android. Bet Marie Laveau never foresaw iPhone apps in her future.

Esoterica Occult Goods

541 Dumaine St.

(504) 581-7711

Its business card positions the shop as "Tools for the Beginner and the Advanced Worker of Ritual Magick." The back of the card states, "Keep Me—I'm Lucky." A card sits in my wallet as I write. No great luck yet, but at least my wallet hasn't been stolen.

The website intones, "The One Stop Shop for all your occult needs."

Owner Lady Mimi Lansou does in-shop readings.

CRYPT ADVISOR

F&F Botanical Spiritual Supply

801 N. Broad St.
(504) 482-9142
HOURS: 8:00 A.M.–5:30 P.M. Mon–Sat, closed Wed
www.orleanscandleco.com

F&F was first called the Kingdom of the Yoruba Religion, and owned by Enrique Cortez, author of *Secretos de la Religion Yoruba*. It was purchased in 1981 and renamed F & F Spiritual Church Supply.

"New" owner (of the last 30+ years) Felix Figueroa had already been selling spiritual candles and supplies around New Orleans for years. F & F has grown to become the largest and most trusted spiritual store in New Orleans for those seriously into voodoo and not merely for kitsch and consumption. Felix's son-in-law, Jonathan Scott, joined the store in 1987.

The products offered on the website are only a small fraction of the more than six thousand items on display in the store. F&F has candles, essential oils, herbs, gift baskets, roots, spiritual books, artisan jewelry, photographs, fragrance oils, Santeria tools, sacred statues of saints and demons, and, for some reason, Mardi Gras beads.

I've watched as people have described their wants or afflictions to Felix and then he turns to his wall of roots and herbs to whip up a concoction to fulfill their needs. In broken English, Felix issues a constant refrain about health. "Everyone wants powder or candles for money and love. Health is where happiness begins."

The shop has the largest assortment of candles I've ever seen. There are candles to help you get a job, candles to help with your court case, ones for money or love, or to keep the law away, to cause a breakup, and my personal favorite, the Do What I Say candle. Like po'boys, candles can come "fully dressed." Dressed candles have been anointed with appropriate oils and herbs. They are twice as expensive, but if you really want people to Do What You Say, it's worth the extra expense.

There are also bath powders for jinx removal, success baths, love baths, and peaceful home baths. And aerosol sprays, with the much needed Gambling Spray before you go to the race track or Harrah's Casino. And those hard-to-find items like a white hair plucked from the second-born fawn of a blessed doe from the North Shore. I forget what the white hair is supposed to do, but it's probably good to have one around "just in case."

There is a reader around back of the shop named Claudia, but she speaks not a word of English. The two times I tried, she was there but her interpreter was not. So, if she said "mucho dinero" I wouldn't have known if she meant I was about to come into big money or if I owed her a bundle. There should be an interpreter available most Fridays and Saturdays.

As one plugged into the community, Jonathan Scott can connect you with a great variety of readers, from macumba style to Santeria or many others.

Hex Old World Witchery
1219 Decatur St.
(504) 613-0558

This is an old-world gift shop for witches and witch-wannabes. Hex sells candles, wands, potions, pendulum boards, potions, wands, jewelry, incense, herbs, voodoo dolls, spell kits, wands, Ouija boards, brooms, statues, and wands. Yes, I know I wrote wands four times. The website seems not to know it has listed them twice.

In store, you can also visit and leave a note at the Witches' Altar of the Dead. Thousands of people each year leave notes on the altars in both Salem and New Orleans and each November, on the night of the witch goddess Hekate, they burn the left-behind notes in honor of those cherished souls.

Island of Salvation Botanica
2372 St. Claude Ave.
(504) 948-9961
www.isleofsalvationbotanica.com

This bright turquoise shop in the bright orange Healing Center is run by Mambo Sallie Ann Glassman, a Jewish girl from Maine. She has been practicing voodoo in New Orleans since 1977. In 1995 she traveled to Haiti to undergo the *couche* initiation rituals and was ordained as Ounsi, Kanzo and Mambo Asogwe, or a high priestess of Vodou. Mambo Sallie Ann is one of the few white Americans to have been ordained through the traditional Haitian initiation.

She has developed a bit of a Deepak Chopra brand with books published by Random House and articles in the *New York Times*, the *New Yorker*, *Los Angeles Times*, the *Wall Street Journal*, and *National·Geographic*, plus appearances on shows like *World News Tonight* and *Pagans Tonight* (a real show).

A wide variety of voodoo novelties are available in her store, many of which have been handcrafted by Sallie Ann Glassman herself. These include two unique sets of tarot cards: the Enochian Tarot is derived from the magical system of Elizabethan magician Doctor John Dee, and a New Orleans Voodoo Tarot that replaces the standard four tarot suits with depictions of the spirits of the major strands of voodoo: Petro, Congo, Rada, and Santeria.

Said Mambo Sallie of her practice, 'It's nonstop twenty-four hours a day. I get people from all walks of life, from street people to professors to psychiatrists to political leaders. They aren't looking for hexes or charms to make someone's nose fall off. It's something much more basic. They turn to voodoo because there's an increasing desperation in our culture for spiritual meaning and direction."

Marie Laveau House of Voodoo
739 Bourbon St.
(504) 581-3751

This store doubles and triples as gift shop, a museum, and a shrine. There are kitschy souvenirs up front and a spiritual advisor in the back, who performs readings just by feeling your pressure points. There's an entire cast of other readers. Rose, Betty, Jennifer, and Miles do palm readings, Hope and Phillip do tarot card readings, Irene does something a card and palm combo, and Darren Bu Care does a Vedic palmistry and tarot combo. The store located next to the only two decent music venues on Bourbon Street, Fritzel's and The Funky Pirate. The other bars pretty much feature bad cover bands doing Journey.

The House of Voodoo used to be the home of Queen Bianca. In life she was a reigning queen of New Orleans voodoo since 1983, when she received the title from Liga Foley, her aunt by marriage and a granddaughter of Marie Laveau. Not to be confused with Queen Bianca Del Rio, a raging queen of New Orleans female impersonators who infamously dismisses her competition with quotes like "It looks like she went into a Claire's Boutique, fell on the sale rack, and said 'I'll take it,'" and when asked if she received any help or advice from other impersonators, replied, "Well, they're all helping me by being horrible and making me look better."

The Museum of Death

227 Dauphine Street
(504) 593-3968
www.museumofdeath.net

The Museum of Death recently opened a branch in New Orleans. The original started in San Diego in 1995 in a building once owned by Wyatt Earp, but they later had to move to Los Angeles after being evicted for trying to recreate the Heaven's Gate cult suicides with beds and clothing acquired from the actual death scene. And here I'm worried about getting back my security deposit because of a knick in the wall!

This is a self-guided tour. After you pay upfront and heed the ticket taker's warning—"It's pretty graphic back there"—you pass through makeshift curtains into the back rooms.

There, you'll find bizarre drawings and letters by mass murderers, a collection of prison shanks (that were used in real murders), skulls, a clearly posed taxidermy snake claimed to be "eating itself," a Ripley's Believe It or Not–like fur-covered fish, a death mask of Adolf Hitler that's obviously been dropped because the Führer's nose is broken off, and a bra and a pair of panties worn on death row by serial killer Aileen Wuornos.

I would have been fine to not see a photo of Nicole Brown Simpson's nearly severed head, but otherwise it's not all that graphic—just a few film loops of autopsies and photos of murder victims.

Overall, the museum feels like a throwback to the days of sideshows and carnival tents. They have a gift shop selling T-shirts, hoodies, and the very desirable Serial Killer Trivia Game.

Founder, J. D. Healy has a lifetime of expertise in the morbid and grotesque. He corrected me that Jayne Mansfield was not decapitated in a car accident just outside New Orleans. She merely lost the top quarter of her skull. J. D. is also in the market to buy and display anything to do with the Axeman of New Orleans, so if you have anything laying around in your attic, let him know.

New Orleans Historic Voodoo Museum

724 Dumaine St.
(504) 680-0128
www.voodoomuseum.com

The New Orleans Historic Voodoo Museum is a small, darkly lit enclave three doors off Bourbon Street. Inside is a musty jumble of wooden masks, portraits of voodoo queens, and a Halloween Superstore's supply of human skulls. Owner and expert is Jerry Gandolfo, a former insurance company manager with a perpetual hangdog expression. He and his brother Charlie set up the business in 1972. At their height, the museum attracted 120,000 visitors a year, including busloads of school kids on field trips.

Gandolfo comes from an old Creole family. His grandparents spoke only French and rarely ventured beyond Canal Street into the "American" part of New Orleans. Gandolfo grew up watching neighbors sweep red brick dust across their doorsteps each morning to ward off hexes, and back then, love potions were sold in local drugstores alongside soda bicarbonate and laxatives.

He grew up hearing stories of how his French ancestors were living in Saint-Domingue (now Haiti) when slave revolts overran their sugar plantation. To save Gandolfo's kinfolk, a loyal slave hid them in barrels and smuggled them to New Orleans. The slave, it turned out, was a voodoo queen. When Gandolfo reached adulthood, he learned practically every Creole family was telling the same lore, so it may lack a certain factual base.

Gandolfo's older brother Charles, an artist and hairdresser, wanted a more stable career. Jerry suggested, "How about a voodoo museum?" Charles—soon to be known as "Voodoo Charlie"—set about gathering a hodgepodge of artifacts of varying authenticity: horse jaw rattles, strings of garlic, statues of the Virgin Mary, yards of Mardi Gras beads, alligator heads, a clay *govi* jar for storing souls, and the wooden kneeling board allegedly used by Marie Laveau.

Charlie presided over the finished museum, always decked out in a straw hat, an alligator tooth necklace, and carrying a staff carved as a snake. "At one point he made it known that he needed skulls, so people sold him skulls, no questions asked," Gandolfo said. "Officially, they came from a medical school."

Outside the museum, Charlie went onto re-create raucous voodoo ceremonies on St. John's Eve (June 23) and Halloween night. He performed

All things Voodoo

at private weddings, which involved snake dances and traditional spirit-summoning drumming.

Voodoo Charlie died of a heart attack in 2001, on Mardi Gras day. His memorial service, held in Congo Square, attracted hundreds of mourners, including voodoo queens in their trademark *tignons*, or head scarves. Jerry Gandolfo, the more knowledgeable but less flamboyant brother, took over the museum, sans straw hat and alligator tooth necklace. Jerry has appeared on numerous radio talk shows and in documentaries and TV shows, including on the Disney Channel. He will forever honor his brother, claiming Charlie "was responsible for the renaissance of voodoo in this city. He revitalized it from something you read in history books and brought it back to life again."

Reverend Zombie's House of Voodoo

723 St. Peter St.

(504) 486-6366

www.voodooneworleans.com

The shop is a double-wide, by far the largest voodoo shop in the Quarter. Right across the street from two New Orleans institutions, Preservation Hall and Pat O'Brien's, Reverend Zombie's will have pretty much everything you need. Its most popular spell kits are Other Attorneys Be Stupid and Hex Your Ex. But Reverend Zombie's also sells cigars, Zippo lighters, tote bags, dream pillows, and very cool T-shirts in 22 original designs.

Voodoo Authentica of New Orleans Cultural Center & Collection

612 Dumaine St.

(504) 522-2111

Brandi Kelley staffs her shop with actual practitioners, not timecard punchers. She stated, "Whether you're a visitor or a local, you've got some place to get free information and to buy something to bring back home that's actually made in New Orleans if you need to do love, health, or prosperity work." This is your one-stop shop for authentic voodoo in the heart of the French Quarter, offering private rituals, consultations, special events services, voodoo dolls, gris-gris bags, potion oils, spiritual art. Brandi opened the shop in 1996 to have a place where she'd be comfortable.

She also hosts the annual VoodooFest, held every Halloween. The free festival's goals are to honor the ancestors, educate the public about this widely misunderstood religion, and to preserve and celebrate the unique spiritual heritage of New Orleans.

Voodoo Spiritual Temple

828 N. Rampart St.

(504) 522-9627

Priestess Miriam presides over this voodoo domain. Some online comments describe her as aloof or even nasty. Others state just the opposite. Clearly, she matches the energy and the spirit of those coming into her space and approaching her. So, don't act like no sassy skeptic or gum-cracking tourist. Her services include consultations, rituals, potions, tours, and lectures. Miss Miriam has been in the movie *Faustbook* and featured in many documentaries and articles in the New York Times and Spin magazine.

Her track record, however, is not 100 percent infallible. She presided over the wedding of Nicolas Cage and Lisa Marie Presley. Their marriage lasted only three months, though who are we to say they didn't enjoy a fabulously happy three months? When the winless Cleveland Browns came to New Orleans to play the Saints on Halloween, a radio station convinced her to do a ritual outside the Superdome to guarantee a Saints victory. On the very last play of the game, Browns quarterback Tim Couch had his one and only shining moment in an otherwise complete bust as an overall #1 NFL draft pick. Couch hurled a voodoo overcoming and appropriately named Hail Mary 55-yard, game-winning touchdown pass. Miriam also did her thing to protect New Orleans from Hurricane Katrina. That didn't work out so well, either.

Yesteryear's
626 Bourbon St.
(504) 523-6603

The store has all the usual assortments of candles, powders, and dolls plus elaborate feathery masks made by owner Teresa Latshaw.

Where Do the Locals Tarot? The Best Readings in New Orleans

Many of the following psychics and voodoo soothsayers have been profiled in earlier chapters, and therefore many entries for readings or root work will be brief. I've chosen to not list any of the many Miss Ivy or Ms. Grace readers with 888 phone numbers "Serving the New Orleans area." There are just too many and you could well be calling some reader sitting in her kitchen in Rockaway, New Jersey.

Bottom of the Cup

327 Chartres St.

(800) 729-7148

The Cup has been doing readings since 1929. Bottom of the Cup is the #1 psychic reading establishment in New Orleans. I am most enamored with Otis Briggs, but they're all good.

Earth Odyssey

306 Chartres St.

(504) 581-1348

The store sells sterling silver designer gemstone jewelry, collectible minerals, and fossil specimens. But, it also has tarot and crystal healing workshops, and you can have a psychic reading performed by Dawn Taylor, who offers tarot, angel, Chinese face and hand, and phoenix readings. "She has an extensive knowledge of gemstones and their properties and can recommend a stone to assist in achieving that which you are seeking."

Elmer Glover

1928 Canal St.

(504) 220-1995

New Orleans' leading *houngan*, or male voodoo priest, is Dr. Elmer Glover, now in his mid-60s and a voodoo practitioner the last 30 years. He has traveled to Haiti, Belize, Brazil, and Africa to immerse himself in voodoo and related animist belief systems like macumba, Santería, and condomblé. Dr. Glover has also run an herb emporium and head shop and was previously a karate instructor at Cho Chi Zen.

His online reviews are passionate (A LOT of capital letters!) but decidedly mixed:

> This guy is the real deal!—this guy Elmer is the real deal! I spent 2 months with him and watched him perform MAGIC!

> A VOO-DOOO practitioner and leader!—ELMER GLOVER knows what he's doing. HE uses ancient techniques that date

back to the secret society that he belongs to. THIS Guy knows his stuff! I have seen it first hand!

ELMER GLOVER IS A FRAUD I WASTED $400 THAT I SENT HIM. BEWARE DONT WASTE YOUR TIME AND MONEY—HE DIDNT DO ANYTHING FOR ME.

ELMER IS A LIER, THEIF, CHEAT, FRAUD, LOCAL TOWN DRUNK.

To quote Hunter S. Thompson, "Buy the ticket, take the ride . . . and if it occasionally gets a little heavier than what you had in mind, well . . . maybe chalk it off to forced conscious expansion: Tune in, freak out, get beaten."

House of the Divine Prince
1921 Josephine St.
(504) 265-1699

The Divine Prince, or Ty Emmecca, offers training and instruction in the arts and of traditional African-based religions and initiation processes, for a minimum fee of $85. He also offers assistance in numerology, personal master numbers and divine numerology for every occasion, for a minimal fee of $85. You can work with him on e-mail and receive a four-page response in Microsoft Word Professional in "font 16" (he's quite specific) for $85. A "complete" reading is $125. You can get specific ceremony initiations for $750. And he provides emergency services for $1,500. But with that, you'll also receive a free toaster oven or food processor. (Kidding!) (About the toaster, but not the price.)

You can now Skype TheDivinePrince. I didn't dare ask the price.

Ava Kay Jones
813 Toulouse St.
(504) 412-0202

Ava Kay Jones was born on Halloween, raised in New Orleans, and an attorney by trade until she found her true path. She has grown to become a leading authority on New Orleans voodoo and African spirituality.

Sidney Smith

Sidney Smith, founder of Haunted History Tours, wasn't the first to offer ghost tours of New Orleans, but his have become overwhelmingly the most popular. He's sort of the Bill Walsh or Bill Parcells of ghost tours; his coaching tree of former Haunted History tour guides have created most of his company's competition and has spawned a ghost tour industry that, if statistics were to be compiled, would probably dust beignets and "Who Dat" T-shirts in bringing tourists' dollars into the city's economy.

Sidney was born and raised in New Orleans. His first career was as a photographer of rock musicians, beginning at the tender age of fifteen. He characterizes Cameron Crowe's *Almost Famous* as virtually his biography. Not old enough to vote or drive a car, barely old enough to shave, Sidney was hanging out with Bruce Springsteen, the Allman Brothers, and local musicians like Ernie K-Doe and seeing his photographs regularly printed in *Rolling Stone*, *Creem*, *Circus*, and other top rock 'n' roll magazines.

His dream photography project became his nightmare. Like so many of his generation (which is also my generation), the Beatles coming to America and appearing on *The Ed Sullivan Show* February 9, 1964, rocked his world. Their sound, their look, everything about them was wildly different from anything that preceded. They created a cultural revolution the likes of which have not been equaled over the past fifty years.

Sidney had worshipped the Beatles for almost ten years when Paul McCartney came to New Orleans to record a new album. After failing to get any response to his attempts to set up a photo shoot with McCartney, Sidney received a phone call out of the blue asking him to bring his portfolio to Le Richelieu Hotel. McCartney's manager, upon seeing and liking Sidney's work, asked him one question:

"When you meet Paul, you aren't going to cry, are you?" They'd worked with other young photographers who'd been so overwhelmed meeting the musical god (remember, they were *"bigger than Jesus"*) they started streaming tears. "Makes Paul a tad uncomfortable when they go all barmy like that."

Assuring the manager he'd remain professional, Sidney was led back to the hotel's swimming pool where Paul and Linda sat with their kids. He got to hang out with his idol while repeating the mantra, "I'm not going to cry, I'm not going to cry."

Sidney was hired on to shoot the album cover and hang out with Paul to capture some candid shots. This included being the only photographer on board when Paul and his buddies—including Duane Allman and Professor Longhair—took a river cruise up the Mississippi. He knew this was a photographer's opportunity of a lifetime and these shots would put him securely on the map. Twenty-year-old Sidney was in Heaven—that is, until the boat returned to dock in New Orleans. Putting down his camera equipment and bags of undeveloped film on deck, he turned a moment later to discover everything had been stolen. It was

Sidney Smith

like Carrie being chosen homecoming queen only to be doused in pig's blood. The experience was devastating. Sidney replaced the camera and lenses, but could never replace the images lost. He dabbled in photography awhile longer, but his heart was no longer in it.

Sidney's next and highly successful gig was delivering singing and/or stripping telegrams. As he noted, "Everything from 'Get Well' to 'Go to Hell.'" Beyond performing himself, he was hiring and training others, plus setting up franchises in other cities across America.

This too came to a dramatic, career-changing end in a single moment. Still in shape in his forties and able to deliver the goods, Sidney was performing at a bachelorette party. Everyone was having a wildly good time until the guest of honor whipped out a twenty-year-old photograph of Sidney performing for her mother. While she undoubtedly thought the picture was sweetly nostalgic, for Sidney it was another bucket of pig's blood. Being a second-generation strip-o-gram performer had not been his vision nor career goal. It was time to hang up the tear-away pants and thong.

Chef Paul Prudhomme has a wonderful quote, "New Orleans is like that. It will nudge you to become the person you were meant to be." After successful but shortened careers as a photographer, then strip-o-gram performer, Sidney was being nudged to become King of Haunted Tours.

About this time, Sidney took a ghost tour from the then-only person offering them. The guide was a crusty old man carrying a lantern around the Quarter. What impressed Sidney the most was how incredibly rude the man was. When one guest asked a question early on, the guide responded, "Is your question just an introductory faux pas, or do you plan to be this stupid the entire tour?" Later, when a different man at the back of the group whispered something to his wife, the guide snapped like the meanest second grade teacher, "Since you seem to want to talk, would you like to come upfront and lead the tour?"

Sidney felt he can do this better. Simply not ridiculing your paying customers would be a start. He went out, studied New Orleans dark history, and scripted what was and still is the city's premier ghost tour, plus vampire tour, voodoo tour, cemetery tour, and recently added a French Quarter history tour.

When Haunted History launched, there were just the two ghost tour companies. Today, there are well over twenty. And they don't always play nice when competing for tourists' dollars. Tearing up or throwing out each other's brochures from travel kiosks and concierge desks is the least of their offenses.

One competitor posts a man with a sign "Ghost Tour Starts Here" about a block from the actual meet up location for Haunted History's tour. Their aim is to intercept and redirect (i.e., steal) Sidney's customers. Another company set up a spy to pretend to want to fill a vacant position at Haunted History. After working there a week, just long enough to memorize Haunted History's tour scripts, he bolted back to his "real" employer. The spy is now a chief officer in a tour company that proclaims they "are tired of 'cookie-cutter' tours." I guess while "cookie-cutter" is bad, stolen recipes are OK.

The Ghost Tour Wars extend beyond fighting amongst themselves. The city's Taxicab Bureau, which licenses and oversees tour guides, has made a concerted effort to make the guides' lives difficult, if not a living Hell. Sidney's night tour groups have been stopped by inspectors who aim flashlights in the faces of tour takers as they count to make sure the size of the group doesn't exceed the 28-person limit. The bureau, specifically their director, Malachi Hull, have been accused of targeting tour guides for harassment. Many guides claim inspectors have been given specific numerical goals by Hull to issue citations to tour guides. The 236 issued in 2013 was upped to a goal of 600 in 2014. The bad blood between tour companies and the Taxicab Bureau finally boiled over when guide Emmanuel Esterlin was pepper-sprayed and handcuffed by bureau inspector Ronnie Blake. Another guide, Wendy Bosma, was in front of the LaLaurie Mansion one night when she was violently tossed against a car by inspector Wilton "Big Will" Joiner as he wrestled away her permit for supposedly not adhering to the mandated 50 foot distance between one tour group and another. Said Esterlin's lawyer, "They don't have the authority to do that [manhandle, handcuff, or pepper spray]. Our position is they're no different than a meter maid." Guides assembled 100 deep in front of City Hall to protest and to demand Malachi Hull be fired.

I asked Sidney if, other than bureau harassment, anything truly weird or scary happened during his tours. He started with some well-worn chestnuts you'll hear time and again. If you take photographs at haunted places like the LaLaurie Mansion or La Pretre House, he said, in about 90% of the pictures will be ethereal gasses or light orbs. There is a single and specific spot outside the LaLaurie Mansion where Sidney has personally experienced five different people fainting and collapsing into a heap. Hundreds have done so in the same spot.

But, he added, he had only one experience that truly made the hairs on his arm stand up. For a tour group he himself guided one night, there was a woman and her young son amongst the tourists. About half way through, the boy left his mother and came upfront to stand by Sidney for the rest of the tour. Sidney kept his eye on the boy, assuring he was perfectly safe. At the end of the tour, the mother in the back started yelling, "My son! Where's my son? He was *just* here!"

Sidney motioned to the boy next to him for the last hour. The mother rushed up, questioning her son.

"How did you get up here? Why did you leave my side?"

The boy answered, "Because you were holding that other boy's hand."

There was, of course, no other boy.

Priestess Ava is also the founder and featured performer of the Voodoo Mkumba Dance Ensemble, an award-winning performance group of drummers, dancers, fire-eaters, and sword and snake dancers. She was the inspiration behind Disney's "Mama Odie" character in *The Princess and the Frog*. Her slogan is that Miss Ava "Digs a Little Deeper."

Maria Shaw Lawson
(810) 631-6887
MariaShawLawson@aol.com

Maria Shaw's columns in *TV Guide*, *Soap Opera Digest*, and the *National Enquirer* have helped create her position as THE psychic to the B-level stars. She has appeared on *The Anna Nicole Show* when Anna was alive and *The Tony Danza Show*, when anyone other than friends and family cared if he was alive. She's become a personal reader for Larry the Cable Guy, Jenny McCarthy, *American Idol*'s Julianne Hough and Chris Daughtry, Lisa Rinna and her lips, *General Hospital*'s Mary Beth Evans, and many cast members from *Days of Our Lives*.

If any of these names cause your heart to flutter, Maria Shaw may be the perfect reader for you when you visit New Orleans. Or, she may be coming to you on her new Soul Mates and Hot Dates; Past lives, Present Loves Tour, selling out in cities like New York, Las Vegas, Los Angeles, and Chicago.

Willow Le Mechant
(504) 377-3308
willowlemechant@yahoo.com

Willow, profiled earlier, is a high priestess of Wicca, ordained minister, and Reiki master. She offers intuitive readings through tarot and palm, with over 35 years of experience. She can also provide spiritual counseling, clearings, and Reiki healing and classes.

Willow is available for parties and events. She offers private readings in her home by appointment and online, via e-mail and chat, and by the time *Fear Dat* is published, her dreamed-for the Divine Source should be up and running.

Metaphysical Resource Center

1708 Lake Ave., Metairie
(504) 708-8353

An all-star cast from which to choose a coveted clairvoyant:

- Alexandria Mazzarino: crystal card reading, astrology, birthdate decoding, chakra balancing
    $30 for 15-minute first-time session
    Chakra balancing $60 for session
    Astrology $75 for 45 minutes; must call with birth information
- AnnMarie Touchette: psychic medium, tarot reader, Hypnotist, and healer
    Psychic medium/combo sitting $50 for 30 minutes, $100 for 1 hour
    Table-tipping séance $45
- Kalila Smith: gestalt/NLP therapist, Reiki healer, intuitive tarot reader
- Sean Rutherford: tarot reader
    $50 for 30 minutes
    $90 for 1 hour
- Sid Patrick: international psychic medium, intuitive tarot reader
    $50 per session
- Tara (McKinney) Faulkner, PhD: destiny astrology, star DNA activation, Mayan soulcode, astrological mediumship
    $20 for 20 minutes + $1 per minute after 20 minutes
- William Corey, psychodynamatist: metaphysical insights, readings, and interpretations
    Individual readings (1 person) $115 per session
    Couple readings (2 persons) $155 per session

Mystic Tea Leaves

638 ½ Royal St.
(504) 523-1063
www.frenchquartervoodoo.com

Catherina Williams has 50 years of experience. All of her sessions are private and held in the strictest confidence. In addition to all the more typical love, money, and past lives guidance, Catherina can also help you with hair loss and hyper children.

Another claim to fame is her holding of the Guinness World Record for the largest voodoo doll ever assembled. The 21-foot 8-inch doll was used for a party where guests pinned wish notes to the fabric-covered Spanish moss doll and Catherina led them in a ritual dance around the doll. I feel quite certain the airlines would require you to check a 21-foot voodoo doll on your return flight home.

Cari Roy

935 Gravier St.
(877) 774-6652
info@neworleanspsychic.com
www.neworleanspsychic.com

Profiled earlier in the book, Cari Roy is, quite simply, the #1-rated psychic in America. And you'll get a hug.

Kalila Katherina Smith

(504) 858-3978
kalila@kalilasmith.com

Kalila is the paranormal-popular "It" Girl. She was one of the founders of Haunted History Tours (her long black–haired images are still used on its posters and brochures), upgraded Erzulie's, and is part of the super staff at Metaphysical Resource Center in Metairie. She is the author of *Journey into Darkness . . . Ghosts & Vampires of New Orleans, Searching for Spirits*, and *Miami Ghosts, Legends, & Mysteries*. Her psychic work on paranormal investigations has been showcased on the Travel Channel, A&E, History Channel, the SyFy Channel, BBC, the Discovery Channel, ID, and MTV. She wrote and directed *Journey into Darkness . . . The Trilogy*, a video documentary.

Voodoo Mystic Haven

(985) 542-1681
voodooluna@gmail.com
www.voodoomystichaven.com

The website opens with a 1,896-word "About Me" section that never once mentions the mystic's name. We learn he or she is a powerful psychic and practitioner of magic, and sells handcrafted authentic New Orleans voodoo spell kits, voodoo dolls, potions, oils, gris-gris bags, and voodoo baths. All are from very powerful recipes of Marie Laveau's. Before reading this site, I had no idea Marie Laveau left behind recipe cards. They must be worth oodles.

Psychic readings go for $150 per hour, but you can get a half-hour for $75. Candles, gris-gris, and spell kits sell for between $35 and $50. But the site accepts only Western Union, money orders, and certified cashier's checks. And then about half of the remainder of the very wordy site emphasizes,

> All items are sold as curios only and for entertainment purposes only . . . Voodoo Mystic Haven can not guarantee results or take responsibility for the outcome of all our magical products, readings, or services. If magical products fail or if the magic does not turn out like you want, Voodoo Mystic Haven is not responsible for the outcome and disclaims all magical products, readings and services . . . Voodoo Mystic Haven can not and will not guarantee 100% of our magical products, readings and services . . . we can not accept exchanges or give refunds NO EXCEPTION. Once you make the order and send payment you will not get a refund for any reason.

I'm getting very strong psychic impressions that these goods may or may not work, but you won't get your money back no matter what.

Alyne Pustanio

apustani@yahoo.com
www.alynepustanio.net

Alyne doesn't do personal readings, doesn't give tours, and other than her books, has nothing to sell you. I list her at the end of this section because she deserves the space. She's a sixth-generation New Orleanian, recognized as a leading expert in the fields of paranormal research, the supernatural, and the occult, and is deeply knowledgeable in the folklore and haunted history of New Orleans. Alyne has been featured on the TV series *Ghost Hunters* and in the History Channel's *Haunted History*. She has also appeared on the Travel Channel, the Discovery Channel, the Destination America Channel, the National Geographic Channel, BIO, and the Golf Channel. I know, I find golf pretty scary, too, but I didn't know others were equally scared by the ever-increasing swarms of sunburned white men.

You can book Alyne for paranormal investigations, lectures, or events by writing to her at apustani@yahoo.com.

In my own amateur-hour wanderings, I have not yet found the desired monkey and cock voodoo curio statue in any of the shops listed. It's a small statue, usually ivory in color, and about the size of a chess piece. The monkey in Yoruban (West African) tradition stands for the trickster. He's able to fool the future and turn it into anything he wants. The cock (A rooster! Get your mind off Bourbon Street!) is the sign of strength and can overcome all obstacles. The statue, depicting their dance together, allegedly has the power to bring the owner good luck and, more important, eliminate any curses on you for three years. At the end of three years, you're required to abandon the statue at a crossroads or grave site, or risk having a world of bad juju heaped upon you. I've heard, but have not seen, the statues are sometimes left at Marie Laveau's tomb. Then, I have also heard when shopping at Sallie Glassman's Isle of Salvation that the whole monkey and cock curio is just some local merchant trying to find additional ways to snooker tourists into parting with their money.

That's the way it is with all our voodoo amulets and practices, plus vampires, plus ghosts. Either you don't believe it, or you do . . . or you spend some time in New Orleans to turn don'ts into dos.

ALEXEY SERGEEV

AFTER(LIFE)WORD

Those who don't believe in magic will never find it. —**Roald Dahl**

Who are you going to believe, me or your own eyes? —**Groucho Marx**

A certain number of readers believed in ghosts, psychics, and spiritualists before picking up *Fear Dat*. Others simply find the otherworldly or dark muses cool but don't necessarily believe any of this, except as entertainment. And there are some who are annoyed by all this hogwash and will have nothing to do with my book.

I don't seek to convince anyone or change a single mind. Probably most people in this country think qigong is about as real as the Tooth Fairy, yet a billion people on the other side of the globe live by it. But I do know what I know. I know I experienced some "presence" the night my father died. Flying down from New York to my parents' home in Hilton Head, I was awakened that night by "something" in the room with me. With a clear voice it said to me quite directly, but without words, "Go be with your mother." Tip toeing into her room, I whispered, "Are you okay?" This led to the most personal, honest, and revealing night of conversation we ever exchanged.

I had an earlier "psychic" experience with my father, too. One late Saturday night when I was at college, I climbed up to the roof of the history building, Elliot Hall, and was considering leaping off the edge. Late teens, early twenties can be awful years with all those chemicals, natural and ingested, coursing through your veins and all those major life decisions (should I major in English or zoology?) pressing down. Obviously, I did not jump. But the next day, my mother opened up our weekly Sunday call-home call with, "What were you doing last night at two A.M.?" I froze. She continued, "Your father sat straight up in bed last night and said, 'Something's wrong with Michael.'" I never revealed a thing to them, but I also never forgot that moment.

Like probably many or maybe most of you, I've had a mess of experiences with psychics and readers. Most of them were pure horse swaddle. Sadly, this includes the vast majority lining Jackson Square here in New Orleans. As a publisher, I've toured with a renowned and best-selling author who claimed to receive messages from the dead. But by the time we hit the third city and I had to endure her well-rehearsed shtick, it took all my resolve not to cut her off in the middle of another "reading."

More recently, another huckster reached me via e-mail. Since I was in the middle of writing *Fear Dat*, I thought I'd give it a go. However, he quickly revealed the depth of his intuitive powers depended on Google. He tried to capture my attention (and $88) by stating I was born on a Monday and he sensed I lived in a city that begins with *N*. His previous e-mail had required I fill out fields stating my birthdate (with year) and phone number (with area code). So, I'd given him all he'd needed to do a quick online check to unleash his psychic intuitions.

Phony psychics piss me off because they smear the whole field. I have experienced people with "real" psychic gifts. I regret those who never experience their gifts, having been turned off by the wealth of phonies.

Mary T. Browne is a "real" psychic. Early on in my career, I had the opportunity to get a free reading by Mary T. because my company had just signed her up as an author. I chose to give my free reading to someone who worked for me. Years later, Mary T. Browne's agent came in to pitch her newest book. Again, a free reading was offered. Skip a free psychic reading once, shame on George Bush. Skip a free reading twice, shame on . . . Well, I went this time.

In my first 10 minutes inside her apartment, Mary T. had named the exact dollar amount from three publishers that had job offers in front of me and she told me to cut off the affair I was having. I was playing with fire. I knew exactly what she was talking about. (Note: This was before meeting my second and permanent wife.)

But after these and other facts were revealed, I finally said, "Okay, you've absolutely convinced me there are ways to gather personal information I don't understand. But I knew everything you've told me before I walked in your door. Tell me something about my future or something I don't know."

She said I have a strong interest in cars (which I don't) or that I had a lot of toy cars as a child (which I didn't). She fumbled around and kept insisting there was some important life lesson for me to learn and it has to do with me and cars. I left her apartment thinking she was just way off on this one.

The next week, I was flying to Amarillo to meet with Western Merchandisers, then one of the most important book distributors in the country. As we descended, I was hit with an OMG moment—and this was before OMG was a part of our lexicon.

Every time I went to Amarillo, which was once or twice a year, I would always drop off Western's buyers after dinner and rush out, alone, late at night, to Cadillac Ranch. There was "just something" about Cadillac Ranch that drew me in like a vortex. It was a thinking spot where, over the years, I'd time and again sat and had Bodhi Tree moments of clarity.

This trip, I couldn't get rid of the buyers fast enough. Jane Love was and is one of my favorite people in the book business. But this night I fidgeted and couldn't wait for her to stop talking about her son and our mutual friends. I had answers to learn from the buried Cadillacs. After dinner, I flew down Route 40, practically sprinted to the cars, and more or less demanded they give up their goods. It took me close to an hour to settle down enough to "receive" their message. But, when it came, it was again that clear, direct voice without words.

I finally "got" why Cadillac Ranch appealed to me in such an intuitive but deep way. Someone, in this case Stanley Marsh and the Ant Farm, had spent a whole lot of money buying 10 vintage Cadillacs. Then an immense amount of blueprint planning and heavy-equipment work went into burying these 10 cars, fins in the air, all at the same angle, all equal distance apart. Apparently all this money and effort was used without anyone's ever once saying, "Now, why the fuck are we doing this?"

The beauty of Cadillac Ranch is (to me) that fact that underneath it all, it makes no sense. It was a vision, either by Stanley Marsh or someone at the Ant Farm, and all focus and effort went toward making that vision real in the real world. No energy was wasted on consequences or justifications.

If you're open to them, there are other forces at play more than the mere fact of gravity or the curse of the being on the cover of Madden EA Sports. Ghosts? Psychics? Voodoo? I can't really say what's real and what's wildly imaginative. But, there's little doubt in my mind that New Orleans is closer to these forces and more in touch with a certain kind of Truth. Are we a vortex? A lei line, as psychic Cari Roy calls it?

From the first day I arrived in New Orleans (May 1983), it seduced me as it has so many others before me and after.

In New Orleans, I found the type of freedom I had always needed.
—**Tennessee Williams**

New Orleans is the city where imagination takes precedence over fact. —**William Faulkner**

I came down here about a month ago and am living in the old French Creole Quarter, the most civilized place I've found in America, and have been writing like a man gone mad ever since I got off the train. —**Sherwood Anderson**

I wound up in New Orleans for all those years and it was a great place, really a catalyst creatively. —**Jimmy Buffett**

I came to New Orleans back in 1994 doing the Interview with the Vampire movie, based on the Anne Rice novel, and fell in love with the city. It got under my skin. Everything was sexy and sultry.
—**Brad Pitt**

If I could put my finger on it, I'd bottle it and sell it. I came down here originally in 1972 with some drunken fraternity guys and had never seen anything like it—the climate, the smells. It's the cradle of music; it just flipped me. Someone suggested that there's an incomplete part of our chromosomes that gets repaired or found when we hit New Orleans. Some of us just belong here.
—**John Goodman**

Everyone who's chosen this place to live knows how seductive it is; the city has almost a vortex feeling about it—it just sucks you in. There's definitely something cosmic going on here.
—**Richard Ford**

New Orleans is like that. It nudges you to be what you need to be.
—**Paul Prudhomme**

Part of the seduction for these celebrities, and for so many others, and for me, has to do with New Orleans' dark side and the city's casual acceptance of these facets. Not only do we think there's nothing strange about tourists lining up to pay $25 to walk around our cemeteries, but please ask residents here if they've ever experienced a ghost. Their responses will often be a ho-hum confirmation like I experienced with Richard, the owner of Magnolia Lane Plantation, or the gum-cracking waitress at Pierre Maspero's, who admitted to me there are disembodied voices chatting among the extra rolls of toilet paper and EMPLOYEES MUST WASH HANDS signs in the women's room of this two-hundred-plus-year-old restaurant.

Someday, ghosts and afterlife experiences may become more PBS and NPR than the Travel Channel's ghost-hunting shows.

If you are not from New Orleans, if you have never been to New Orleans,

I hope this book helps draw you here as if fulfilling a pilgrimage to the Wailing Wall or a journey to Lhasa, Tibet. For those of us whom love this city, it's that kind of place.

While writing the manuscript for *Fear Dat*, I passed through Father's Day. Other cities celebrate Father's Day with a hearty Sunday brunch and maybe a one-day sale at Sears' Tool Center. Here in New Orleans on the most recent Father's Day we had a Zydeco Festival and the World Naked Bike Ride.

Here the cray-cray is every day. In New Orleans, we take the *para* out of *paranormal*.

Come join us.

ANGUS MORDANT

ACKNOWLEDGMENTS

Irst, last, and pretty much everything in between, I must thank my wife, Marnie Carmichael. There is no one with whom I'd rather drown at a leisurely pace. When we met, I was hauling in absurd amounts of money as a publisher, plus free limo rides, and a private bathroom in my office that I never used. Well, I used it once. But when people came into my office, calling out "Michael? Michael? He was *just* here!" I couldn't think of an elegant way to flush and reappear, so I stayed in there until they left. I never used my private bathroom again.

Marnie and her self-created, self-run business had already been featured in a *Vanity Fair* piece, "*The Grand Marnie*," plus the *New York Times*, *Elle Decor*, *Food & Wine*, *Bon Appétit*, and *Gourmet*, she'd been on the *Today Show* and the Food Network, and was shortly to be chosen as an Oprah's "Favorite Thing." It seemed like we had a private compartment on the Glam Train.

But our train was about to fly off the tracks. Sometimes we think a voodoo curse has been put on us. More often we simply think life can throw crap at you that you never see coming. We live by an Anne Lamott quote, "There's your plans and there's God's plan, and your plans don't matter." But we also adhere to Charles Bukowski's "Sometimes you just need to pee in the sink."

In the acknowledgments of *Eat Dat*, my previous book, I thanked my editor, Ann Treistman; my publisher, then Kermit Hummel; my then publicist, Tom Haushalter; and all the people of Countryman Press and W. W. Norton. I was especially impressed with the smarts and the charm of Kristin Keith, Norton's regional sales manager.

They all worked (are working) just as hard to bring *Fear Dat* to life.

Even though he has left as publisher to pursue a medical career, I wish to thank Kermit Hummel for his support and efforts on behalf of *Eat Dat*, *Fear Dat*, and setting the foundation for the third book, *Hear Dat*.

I will isolate Ann Treistman, my editor, here because she's been the most intimately and intensely involved with the book. When Ann contacted me in May 2013 to write *Eat Dat*, it was almost like a "call" in the larger sense. After 32 years in the book business, I was no longer with a publisher. I had shuttered my own literary agency. I'd become sort of a book version of a Ronin. Ronin were samurai warriors who had lost their masters and thereby much of their purpose. I was a book person with no books to package, present, or publish. Writing these Dat books about the city I love has, in many ways, brought me back from the dead. Whether one person or tens of thousands read *Fear Dat*, I had the pleasure of writing it and meeting people like Cari Roy and Arthur Raymond Smith, visiting places like Magnolia Lane Plantation, and having a reason to bolt out of bed at 4:00 A.M. to write for an hour or two before I needed to go to a paying gig.

I wish to thank my new editor, Dan Crissman (Ann was promoted to Grand Pooh-Bah), and my new publicist, Devorah Backman, whom I've "known" for just a few introductory emails at the time I write this. Dan's editorial touch was light, direct, and in each case made the manuscript better. Devorah has been wickedly fast in responding to my every request. You can probably guess that some of my requests play at the borders of what one might call "reasonable."

There were also many friends who served as coconspirators, feeding me tips and tidbits about especially ghoulish places and tales. I will call out Beth Spalding and Sylvia Sharp, who have been the most helpful.

I want to use this space to thank the people who helped my first book, *Eat Dat, after* its publication and whom thereby I couldn't acknowledge in that earlier book.

Tom Lowenberg and Judith Lafitte of Octavia Books, for hosting my first book signing. Briton Tice, Amy Loewy, and Ted O'Brien of Garden District Book Shop, for hosting an author panel about New Orleans food and then hosting me in their book tent at Jazz Fest. Rachel Billow, for getting more people to come to the Garden District signing by serving from her food truck, La Concinita. Gladin Scott of Maple Street Books, for successfully hosting a third Uptown bookstore signing by luring in an audience with free food and beer. Cam Boudreaux, for providing his brilliant po'boys as the free food at the signing. Susan Larson, who used her immense powers and "immenser" charms to get me onto a Tennessee Williams Festival panel. Jim Davis, for getting me on a panel at the Louisiana Book Festival. Blythe Danner look-alike Jackie Bullock, for putting me on WRBH radio and Amy C. Sins, for conducting the radio interview with me and later doing a calas demo with me at the Food Festival. Dottie Belleto, president of New Orleans Convention Company, Inc., who got me into Food Fest and has helped Eat Dat in a myriad of other ways, plus Brianna Bell, also with NOCCI, who served as my go-to, get-it-done person, and John Robertson, another NOCCI staff member who tossed off more good ideas and great cheer than a hound dog does fleas. Cara Banasch at the New Orleans Convention & Visitors Bureau. Humid Haney and Mandy Thomas, for carrying *Eat Dat* in Dirty Coast, a T-shirt store as unique as New Orleans itself, and hosting a signing at its Magazine Street location. Lisa Jones, the utterly soulful proprietor of A Tisket A Tasket, a gift basket shop, who propped me right on Decatur Street to sign books during the French Quarter Festival. Walter Gallas, for including me in his event, Vino on the Bayou, at the Pitot Plantation House. Gretchen Erickson, for letting me join its chef and could-be stand-up comic, Kevin Belton, in a demo and signing event at the New Orleans School of Cooking. Dianna Knost, owner of the very cool AKA Stella Gallery, for supporting *Eat Dat* not only in her shop, but buying one copy for each of her gal pals at her 40th birthday party. Virginia Olander, for placing a copy in every one of her Luxury Rentals properties. Lloyd Runyan, for slipping a copy in the backseat pocket of his town cars and limos at Riverbend Charters & Tours. Becky Guillot, for getting placement in the New Orleans Historical Society, and for being an effervescent soul who cheers my spirit, like the ex-Saints cheerleader she was, whenever I bump into her at an Uptown confection shop. Devra Dedeaux, another bigger than life spirit (kind of common here in New Orleans), who runs Cunningham Enterprises and got *Eat Dat* into Pop City, Fun Rock'n, and other cool area gift shops. Sylvia LeBlanc who supported *Eat Dat* at her Roux Royale culinary gift shop. Sally Buchman, for stocking my book at the historic Roosevelt Hotel. Rosemary James and Joe Desalvo, for hosting a book party in their home, which was formerly William Faulkner's home. Michele, Greg, and the Freret Market staff, where I sold more books than any other venue. My landlady, Tania Hahn, who continuously bought copies to give to her friends and staff, and even allowed me to pay partial rent with signed books. Mary Bonadona, on Tania's staff, who always greets me with a smiling face and shining thoughts when I drop off my rent check. Interviewers Jeff Rivera at Examiner.com and Eric Olsson on his Red Beans & Eric blogsite, and reviewers, particularly Lena Tabori, who gave *Eat Dat* a massive boost when her Huffington Post piece rated it the #1 "Essential" book to read before coming to New Orleans. Lianna Patch of *New Orleans Living*, Mona Hayden in *Louisiana Roadtrips*, Chere Cohen, who writes book columns for practically "everyone" in Louisiana, and a really nice mention in the most unlikely place for *Eat Dat* (but perfect for *Fear Dat*), Suzanne Johnson's *Paranormal Unbound*.

I wish to highlight Mike Zibart, who allowed me to attach a personal essay, "Drowning in Butter & Bacon Fat," to the review on the pages of his Bookpage. Emeril Lagasse for his front-cover blurb. Anne Rice for her laudatory shout-out on her website. And I thank Anne Rice again for agreeing to open this book with her "Fore-warned." And people I don't know, like Jackson Herod, who wrote "This is without a doubt, my favorite book about food that i've ever read" on Amazon.com and Jamie on Goodreads, who commented, "This the best travel book about food I've ever laid hands on." I swear I neither know nor have ever met Jackson or Jamie.

It takes a village to raise a book up from the oblivion of the remainder pile.

INDEX